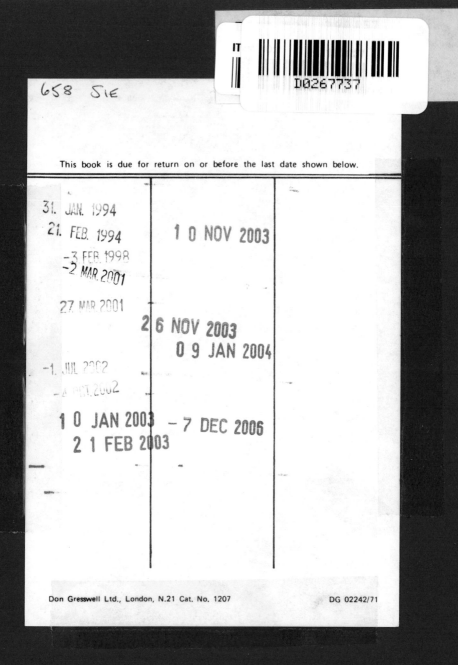

MARCUS SIEFF
ON
MANAGEMENT

MARCUS SIEFF
ON
MANAGEMENT
The Marks & Spencer Way

WEIDENFELD & NICOLSON
LONDON

To my wife Lily
for her continuing
patience and encouragement

CONTENTS

ACKNOWLEDGEMENTS

I wish to thank my secretary, Sharon Tossell, who has been very patient and most helpful; Roger Saoul and Laura Harper for their research; and Alex MacCormick for her advice. I thank Sir Hector Laing of United Biscuits, Per Gyllenhammer of Volvo, and Sir Frank Lampl and Roger Mabey of Bovis for their help.

I also acknowledge the stimulation I got from the books *Making it Happen* by Sir John-Harvey Jones, published by Collins; *The I.B.M. Way* by Buck Rogers, published by Harper & Row; *In Search of Excellence* by Thomas J. Peters & Robert H. Waterman Jr.; *Made in Japan* by Akio Morita, with permission to reproduce copyright material from William Collins Sons & Co. Ltd; and *The 100 Best Companies to Work for in the U.K.* by Bob Reynolds, published by Fontana.

one

FIRST THOUGHTS

This book is based on my personal experiences of some fifty-five years in business from 1934 to 1989. I have spent the greatest part of my working life in Marks & Spencer. Most of what I have learned about the business world I learned there, beginning as a junior trainee in 1934 and becoming chairman and chief executive in 1972. I retired in 1984.

However, I also learned valuable lessons elsewhere, for many firms supply Marks & Spencer with goods and ever since the days when we were a family firm we have maintained close relations with our suppliers. This was partly because we encouraged and mutually benefited from a close, friendly partnership with them and partly because it has always been our policy to work with those who thought our principles were correct and sensible. They shared our view that good human relations at work were essential for long-term success as were the high quality and good value of the goods they produced and the services they provided. Where our suppliers did not initially carry out such a policy, we discussed with them how they could achieve these aims once they had been agreed.

This meant getting to know a great deal about their methods of running their businesses. If, after a reasonable amount of time, a supplier would not or could not come up to the standards we sought, we discontinued our association. In my time I worked closely with many Marks & Spencer suppliers in the UK and abroad, mainly in the fields of clothing and food, as well as with those firms concerned with the building of our stores and with providing us with services such as transport and warehousing.

I also had dealings at home and abroad with the providers of raw materials to our suppliers of finished goods, and, through our technologists and scientists, with the staffs of various scientific and technological institutions. I worked, too, with a number of organizations concerned with the creation of employment, further development of free enterprise, and with the promotion of good human relations at work generally. This means that I have had the benefit of a wider experience of industry and commerce than one might anticipate from a lifetime working in one firm.

I also learned a great deal in the Army, serving throughout the Second World War, mainly in the Middle East, North Africa, Sicily and Italy, particularly from my duties as an officer in charge of the landing of men and equipment on beaches and in ports in the battle zones of the three theatres of war. There is much that is admirable in the way the services conduct their affairs, particularly in the field of man management – what is not so good has its messages also – and being in action under fire teaches one fundamental lessons about human nature.

Six years ago I gave up all executive responsibilities in Marks & Spencer, retired from the board and became the honorary president of the company. This has enabled me to accept invitations to diversify into activities which have taught me fresh lessons in different spheres: as chairman of *The Independent*, a new and, in the view of many people, I am happy to say, a very fine quality newspaper, one of the best anywhere; a member of the board of Wickes, the DIY chain; chairman of the London subsidiary of the First International Bank of Israel; and a director of the recently established Sock Shop chain. These experiences have not only taught me new lessons but have also confirmed the oldest: that you are never too old to learn – a lesson I recommend not only to seventy-six-year-olds like myself but also to seventeen-year-olds and all age groups in between.

Many people have to learn their early lessons the hard way, and I continue to marvel at the public spirit, faith in human nature and idealism manifested throughout their careers by successful businessmen who had many obstacles to overcome in their youth. By contrast, I was lucky. I learned about the business world at the feet of two outstanding men whose business ethos was their belief not that God helped those who helped themselves but that God helped those who helped their fellow men. If I had to say who has most influenced my attitude to business I would name my father, Israel Sieff, and his lifelong friend, intimate colleague and brother-in-law, my uncle Simon Marks. My father had the gift of teaching by precept and my uncle by example. They were my chief mentors.

They not only taught me the principle of good, responsible, socially valuable and profitable business, but familiarized me with the human face of capitalism and inducted me into sound business practice; they gave me faith in what successful business could do to help the community. This was important to me. At the time when I started to learn how to be a shopkeeper, business and industry were under a cloud of despair and guilt, largely because of the very high level of unemployment growing and persisting throughout the 1920s and reaching its peak in the early 1930s, creating widespread poverty, ill-health and suffering, and in the body politic a decline in belief in democracy. Many young people who might in different conditions have been enthusiastic about going into business were repelled by the idea. They saw the world of commerce as a world to be avoided, if not renounced; hence strong left-wing political views and Communism. It is not difficult to understand why so many people held such views in those days.

Thanks to my family background I had a different view of the business world. I was more sanguine about its values and prospects. So far as prospects were concerned, my optimism was strengthened by what I saw of the early work of an organization called Political and Economic Planning (PEP, now part of the Policy Studies Institute), of which my father was co-founder and chairman of its industry group, later chairman of the whole organization. PEP was a voluntary organization which took the form of a continuing conference, meeting at regular and frequent intervals, drawing together enlightened business, industrial, academic and union leaders, forward-looking politicians of all parties and influential publicists, in all about a hundred strong. They met to consider and implement proposals for bringing down unemployment and generally getting British industry back on its feet. Blueprints were drawn up for them in consultation with their expert permanent staff led by Kenneth Lindsay. Men of the calibre of Maynard Keynes, William Beveridge, Harold Macmillan, Hugh Gaitskell and Walter Citrine, the left-wing head of the Trades Union Congress, all worked together. Studying their activities gave me a vision of what British industry was capable of if properly led and motivated.

These men collaborated irrespective of their political views. Their reports were published as PEP broadsheets; many were first-class, but too few were acted upon. Some years ago Harold Macmillan, then in his mid-eighties, took me to lunch and said, 'You know, Marcus, if we had only implemented many more of the recommendations by PEP and your father in those early days before the Second World War, how much better in many ways our country would have been now. We would have greatly improved our economy, at the same time reducing unemployment and the social and economic miseries which accompanied it.'

Studying my father and my uncle gave me high hopes of what British industry could do to be profitable, more efficient and socially responsible, and of what human beings could and would do for each other if they were given the opportunity. Outstanding, in my youthful experience, was the day when the vicar of a small

South Wales mining town named Mountain Ash wrote to Marks & Spencer, then perhaps better known for its shirts than for its charity. He asked what was the minimum price for a large number of shirts for the very many unemployed miners in his parish. It would, he said, do much for the morale of these brave men if, for the first time in years, they could have a new, whole, unpatched shirt on their backs. My father and uncle arranged to send a consignment of our shirts as a gift, but, by mistake, the shirts were accompanied by the invoice meant for our internal records. The vicar assumed that the invoice was a bill for him and promptly paid it, 'gladly' he said, because it was a joy that such men could get such good shirts at such low prices. His cheque was sent back to him, of course, and his appreciation has become part of the history of Marks & Spencer.

It is one of my first memories of both the company and of business, and it taught me that a successful business which looks after its employees and shareholders also has a responsibility to the wider community and is proud of acting accordingly.

You learn most in business from your own experiences, but there is much to learn from others. I do not claim that what I have seen, taken part in and achieved in business will work equally well for you. I do not know who you are or what you wish to do. I would be surprised, though, if you were able to say at some future date that most of what I recommended to you, when you applied it in practice, let you down. Sound principles do not change, though sound policy often must. Principles are sacrosanct – policy must be flexible. I hope that what I offer will help the aspiring businessman* however young or old, at what-

---

* This word is used in the generic sense including business women. Masculine terminology is used only to avoid clumsy or confusing sentence constructions and is in no way intended to underestimate the important role of women at every level in business.

ever level he finds himself, in big organizations or small, to think more clearly and more imaginatively about what he is doing, could do or should do.

One of the most pleasant aspects of the world of business and industry today is that the careers it offers are demonstrably attracting many more of our able and responsible young people than ever before. It was not so when I went into Marks & Spencer in the early 1930s; at that time for many young people of character and intelligence business did not beckon, and profit was a dirty word.

There were many reasons for this. Firstly, in spite of the Industrial Revolution and the prosperity it created for many – it created poverty too – there was an aristocratic prejudice against those who made money out of trade. Some impoverished land-owners married their sons to the daughters of wealthy steel-masters, but were not keen to have their in-laws to dinner. Secondly, though in the nineteenth century there were some enlightened and humane employers who treated their employees well, there were many hard men who treated their workers badly. As happens in many walks of life, it is the rotten apple in the barrel which gets the publicity. Thirdly, at the end of the nine-teenth century and during the first three decades of this one, the image of business was further clouded by mass unemployment, which began to look like a permanent and necessary characteristic of modern capitalist society. Fourthly, there was also cultural and educational prejudice against business and industry. Many intellectuals looked down on business leaders as philistine or predatory, or both, and some of them expressed this attitude in public. Teachers in schools, conscious of children coming to lessons with holes in their shoes and without proper winter clothing, raised their voices. Clergymen, seeing the suffering and deprivation in the homes they visited pastorally, quoted those passages in the Scriptures which seem to condemn the souls of those who labour in the vineyards for gain. (There are many passages, especially in the New Testament, which contain the contrary message, for instance the much debated parable of the talents in Matthew 25:14–30.) Politicians across the spectrum from naive to disruptive used the shortcomings of business and industry to disseminate propaganda to the effect that private enterprise produced misery for the vast majority and that only in a Socialist society could all men and women be sure of physical and cultural well being.

The experience of the Second World War, which taught many of us that democracy could not prevail against tyranny unless it were armed with the tools of superior industrial might, had salutory lessons for us. But even in the post-war decades there was a strong tendency to regard business as an opening desirable only for boys and girls who had not made the top grade academically. Large and enlightened firms found it difficult to attract promising university graduates and had to resort to sending teams of recruiters around places of higher learning in order to do so, with limited success.

Fifteen years after the war, when I served as a member of the Cambridge University Appointments Board for three years from January 1959, I was shocked to find that the board rarely recommended any interviewee to take up a career in business or industry. This was no oversight; it was a sign of the times. The most able people were recommended to try for the Foreign Office or, failing that, certain other Government departments. It was considered reasonable to take up medicine or an academic career, then came such professions as the law. Hardly any were recommended to go into engineering or industry, and God forbid that anybody should be a shopkeeper like me.

This attitude to business and industry has changed much in recent years. To see that it has done so you need only visit most bookshops and look at the display of books dealing with all aspects of business and, most significant of all perhaps, the number of best-sellers written by successful businessmen. You would not have seen such an array thirty years ago, I can assure you; and in the year in which I left Cambridge to start work in the Marks & Spencer warehouse at Hammersmith Broadway in London there would have been very few, if any, business titles on bookshop shelves.

There are many other indicators of the changed attitude to business and industry. Courses, including degree courses, in business and industry abound at universities, colleges and polytechnics. Evening classes were always available in such studies, but not on the scale they are today. Then there is the Open University on television. Our leading national banks boast of their ability and readiness to advise people how to start their own businesses, and generally but not always give them financial assistance. When I was a young man, the banks seemed inclined to sit there and wait until the young entrepreneur came along with some money he had made. Government departments have developed advisory facilities to help business beginners and are now able, if their proposition looks likely to succeed, to help them with money. The whole atmosphere is different from when I first joined Marks & Spencer.

Some of the reasons for this change in attitude to business and industry seem obvious even to someone like me. Today far more people see that business and industry are not only valuable in themselves but support the worlds of education and culture to a degree which could make life in these spheres far more difficult without them. Through taxes paid by those employed, by direct contributions to universities, hospitals and the arts, and by large sponsorships of all kinds of worthwhile causes, business and industry have initially replaced the patronage once practised by

Renaissance princes. Business and industry continue to make substantial cash contributions to the various provisions for the nation's health and well being.

Another factor, I believe, which has changed our national attitude to business is our awareness of the great efforts made by some of our leading firms to improve human relations in industry, an activity in which I am proud to say Marks & Spencer has been a leader from its early days.

For all these and other reasons business is now established as a worthwhile career for many of the most able of our youth. Profit is no longer a dirty word and the slow but continuing elimination of the 'Us and Them' syndrome is seen as the main way to rid the world of the so-called class war.

The change in the country's attitude to industry and business has never been so apparent as it has in the years since Margaret Thatcher became Prime Minister. She more than anyone has established the ethic and attractiveness of a career in business or industry, and their essential role in the life of British society. I marvel at what she has achieved in this area in such a short time.

It is exhilarating for me to try to transmit some of the experience I have gained during my happy and fulfilled life as a businessman in order to encourage others to carry on better and quicker than I have done what I regard as a worthwhile torch. I am glad that fate made me a shopkeeper. A major part of my job has been to obtain desirable products of good value and quality, and then sell as many of them as I could across the counters of Marks & Spencer. This means that there are many areas of economic activity of which I have some knowledge. It also means, however, that as a shopkeeper I have spent the major part of my life dealing with *people*. Ultimately, whatever the form of economic activity in question, it is *people* that count most. Consequently, it is mainly people that this book is about: not how to manage them, direct them or exploit them, but how to work with them – suppliers, customers and fellow employees alike. I hope that my observations and anecdotes may help readers to enjoy their experience in business as much as I have mine.

two

STARTING YOUR OWN BUSINESS

The most important thing about a business is the quality of people who work in it, from those at the top running the business to the most junior employees. Whatever the business, it is only as good as the people who manage it and work in it.

There are certain essentials if one is to start up or maintain a successful business. I learned early in my business life that the first is to identify products, goods or services for which there is a demand, preferably a growing or unfulfilled demand, and to consider how one can satisfy that demand at a reasonable profit. No matter how high the quality and how good the value of the products or services offered, if there is little or no demand the business will not be successful.

I also learned that today no commercial operation will be successful in the long term if it is not based on certain principles. Policies may change, but principles are, or should be, sacrosanct.

I have found that principles in business cover a wide area; I list below those I consider most important and which I have followed in my own business life:

(i) Perhaps the most important of all is a policy of good human relations with all concerned in and with the operation – employees, customers and suppliers.

(ii) To offer customers goods and services which they want and which should be of high quality and good value.

(iii) To work closely with suppliers and encourage them to use the most modern, efficient techniques of production and quality control dictated by the latest discoveries in science and technology.

(iv) To simplify operating procedures so that the business is carried out in an efficient manner.

(v) To ensure that those in management are not isolated or in water-tight compartments and that, while an individual's responsibility (other than the chief executive's) may be limited to a particular area or areas, he or she should have general knowledge of the operation as a whole.

(vi) Never forget the importance of satisfying the customer.

(vii) To seek wherever possible a source in the United Kingdom.

Much will be said later about the application of these seven principles, but at this stage I want to make some points about the origin and early growth of a successful enterprise.

Even for people who are not in business themselves, the story of how a successful business began, especially if it has grown into a big business, is one of the most interesting things about it, and for people who consider starting their own business the history of origins is important reading.

Before answering the question of how successful businesses originate, here are a few examples from which the reader may care to deduce some of the answers for himself.

I begin with what I know best, the case of my own family. My paternal grandfather, Ephraim Sieff, left Eiregola in Lithuania, part of the Russian dominated Pale of Settlement, at the age of eighteen in 1884 to escape persecution. He paid for a ticket to New York, but a dishonest ticket-seller gave him a ticket valid only as far as Hull, then the main port of North-East England. From Hull my grandfather made his way to Manchester, where he had the good luck to meet up with a woman, another immigrant, who had worked for his parents in Eiregola. She was married to a successful tailor, also an immigrant. She and her husband welcomed my grandfather into their house, and he lived there for several weeks.

She was proud of the way her husband had established himself and showed my father over their house. When they came to the basement where the tailor did his work, my grandfather saw that the floor was littered with a mixture of cuttings, wool, linen and cotton. Back in his homeland my grandfather had served an apprenticeship in the textile industry.

'What do you do with these cuttings?' he asked his hostess.

'Nothing,' she replied. 'They are a waste. We pay a man a few shillings to take them away.'

My grandfather said, 'If I take them away without charging you anything, can I have your cuttings?'

'You are a friend,' she said, 'you can have them on the same terms as he does.'

My grandfather then asked, 'Do you know the name of any firm that might want them?'

'Yes, there's a firm called Beaumont here, they might be interested.'

My grandfather thereupon set to work, using the knowledge he had acquired during his apprenticeship, and carefully sorted the scraps into their different categories and qualities. He borrowed a handcart and took the cuttings to Beaumont, finding his way by means of pieces of paper on which the tailor's wife had written the names of streets and speaking his few words of English. The buyer at Beaumont was impressed with grandfather's scraps and the way they had been sorted, paid him for them, and told him he would take more if the quality was as good. Grandfather made sure it was. From this beginning he steadily built up one of the best scrap businesses in Britain and in time became a wealthy man. Mr Beaumont had no heir and in due course my grandfather became his partner, and the firm became Sieff & Beaumont.

That is the story of how my paternal grandfather got started in business in Britain. Now for the story of my maternal grand-father's commercial beginnings in this country. At about the same time as Ephraim Sieff arrived in Manchester, Michael Marks, a Jewish immigrant from Bialystok in what was then Russian Poland, also a refugee from Russian persecution, came to Leeds to seek employment at Barran's Clothiers, who gave work to immigrants from Eastern Europe. The eighteen-year-old Michael walked slowly down the main street in Kirkgate repeating the only English name he knew: 'Barran's.'

On his way he came across Isaac Dewhirst, a leading Methodist, who was a small manufacturer and wholesale merchant of haber-dashery items which he sold to shops, market stalls and pedlars. Hearing this lad asking for Barran's, he befriended him and lent him £5 – a lot of money in those days – which my grandfather spent on stocking a tray with goods from Dewhirst, which he then peddled in the countryside. His health was not good enough for him to continue doing this, so he invested his tiny profits in a stall in the open market, on which he displayed a variety of goods with the slogan 'Don't ask the price, it's a penny'. That stall was part of the beginnings of Marks & Spencer; another part was the slogan. Marks & Spencer's turnover with Dewhirst in 1988 exceeded £76 million at cost and are now Dewhirst's largest customer by far; they have been trading together continuously for 105 years.

At almost the same time as my grandfather arrived in Britain, a certain Mrs Annie Desmond was living obscurely in the small village of Claudy in County Londonderry. She had a problem: thirteen children to feed and clothe. In Londonderry, eight miles away, there was a shirt manufacturer, Tillie & Henderson. Annie made an arrangement with them to let her have the cut pieces once a week, which she then distributed to girls living in the village who could sew, taking the finished garments back to the shirtmakers. She bought a pony and trap; then expanded by buying Singer sewing machines, and hiring them to the girls; then, to eliminate unnecessary travel, she brought the girls into her house. The business expanded. A factory was built, named Desmond's, providing much needed employment. Annie, who was clearly a remarkable lady, died prematurely at the age of forty-eight, but the business was carried on by her husband and second eldest son, the father of the present chairman/chief executive, Annie's grandson.

In 1884 in Edinburgh, on the death of his father, Robert McVitie inherited a baker's shop. He saw little prospect of expansion in cakes or bread, but he believed there was a great future for biscuits, which would travel and keep. He went to Europe and later to America to learn more about biscuits, absorbing information which he applied successfully in Edinburgh. That was the origin of McVitie & Price, which grew into United Biscuits, now one of the biggest and finest enterprises of its type in the world, still going from strength to strength under the distinguished and outstanding leadership of Sir Hector Laing; but more about United Biscuits later.

On Christmas Day 1985 Chris Allen and Mark Tomlin met in the Royal Oak public house in Stevenage. Introduced by mutual friends, they soon discovered that they shared an interest in the potential for supplying goods to such developing groups of small shops such as Sock Shop, Tie Rack and Body Shop. Their aim was to produce an item or market an existing item of clothing in a new way which would have a popular demand, would be of good quality, but could be sold at a modest price. Chris left his job as an office furniture salesman and Mark gave up his job as a trainee chef. They began to consider what would be the right item for them to produce.

In June 1986 Chris went for a holiday in Greece and Mark planned to follow him, hoping that a break in the sun would give them an opportunity to look at the future more objectively. Just as Mark was about to leave for Gatwick airport, the telephone rang; Chris had suddenly returned home. He had found that on the beaches in Greece everybody was wearing boxer shorts as underwear, beachwear and leisurewear – not only men, but women as well. What he had seen gave him a great idea. They went to the local market in Luton, where they bought samples of as many striking fabrics as they could afford. Chris's mother made them into boxer shorts. They showed them to their friends, who bought them immediately.

The Training Commission (formerly the Manpower Services Commission) offered them financial assistance under the Enterprise Allowance scheme, which gave them a net wage of £40 per week, but they had to put up £1,000 of their own to plough into the business. Initially, they telephoned round and knocked on doors, but no one of consequence wanted to see them; so with samples of pink-pig pattern boxer shorts they went round to Sock Shop, prepared to spend a day waiting there until they had a chance to pass their package of shorts to the buyer. In fact as soon as they made themselves known the buyer came out to see them, and they went away with an order for 1,500 pairs. An order for a further 12,000 soon followed. Their business with Sock Shop, for whom they produce some exclusive designs, is now considerable. Since then they have designed for Top Man, Concept Man, Burtons and Chelsea Girl.

They named their company Revenge and, at the time of writing, two and a half years later, they have 5,000-square feet of factory with modern cutting tables and employ nearly sixty people, including two designers and an accountant. They not only sell to well-known chains in the United Kingdom, but also export to half a dozen countries overseas. Revenge's first year's turnover was more than £1 million, and they have extended their range to include Bermuda shorts, beach shorts, T-shirts and briefs. Their success has come about as a result of meeting an unfulfilled demand for products that represent quality and value.

How successful businesses came to be started has always interested me and the variety of reasons for their coming into existence is in itself an education about business. Take the Abbey National Building Society, for example. It is the biggest building society in the UK with a high reputation; its assets are so extensive that, if it were a bank, it would be one of the hundred biggest banks in the world; and many people would regard it as a citadel of capitalist society, but it was in fact set up by the nineteenth-century radical reformers Cobden and Bright as a means of political progress towards universal suffrage. Their plan was that the funds would be used to buy land, which would then be sold in small parcels to the buyers, who became forty-shilling freeholders and thereby eligible to vote. In turn, the representatives they elected to Parliament hastened the process of reform.

A striking feature of British business is the number of enterprises which have been founded by men and women who were concerned for their fellow human beings – Cadbury Schweppes, for example. In 1824, John Cadbury established a small business to produce cocoa and chocolate; in the 1870s he moved his flourishing business to Bournville, a suburb of Birmingham. From the beginning the Cadburys were highly responsible employers, not only building houses and amenities for their workers, but spending money and imagination on providing the best possible working conditions.

It is no accident that some of Britain's most successful businesses have been established by high principled Quakers, outstandingly the Rowntree family, now manufacturing a fifth of all the sweets and chocolates consumed in Britain today. The fortunes of the firm and the family began in 1752 in York, where a Quaker woman, Mary Tuke, opened a grocer's shop, and later married a man called Rowntree. They prospered, but the great expansion came more than a century later when their successors started to expand the chocolate side of their business to satisfy the growing demand for chocolate due to the rapid increase in the number of working-class people who could afford to buy it. Much of the success of Rowntree was due to their perception of and response to *social* as well as economic change.

This is also true of many other great firms. To begin with a famous American example. After Lavoisier (acclaimed by some as the founder of modern chemistry) had been sent to the guillotine during the French Revolution, one of his former pupils named Du Pont went to America. Eventually Du Pont's firm became an industry in itself. Fifty years ago one of its chemists, Carothers, invented nylon. Today Du Pont produces a vast variety of important substances which have become household words and meet a wide variety of social needs, including Teflon for non-stick cooking pans, Lycra for stretch swimsuits, Kevlar fibres for tyres and many other products.

In 1792 the Smith family started London's first newspaper delivery round, but their great move forward was the result of anticipating the social and economic consequences of the construction of railways, as a result of which they set up stalls to sell newspapers and books inside railway stations, later moving to shops adjacent to them.

There is some similarity between the origins of W.H. Smith and J. Sainsbury. In 1869 John James Sainsbury married the daughter of a dairyman and set up a dairy of his own in North London. After a while, having observed the effects of the growing local railway networks and increasing suburban development, he shrewdly broadened his activities into groceries.

It would be difficult to exaggerate the importance of perception of potential opportunities created by social change either for the founders of new businesses or for entrepreneurs running relatively successful, well-established businesses. Of the latter, one of the clearest examples I know is what Simon Marks and my father did for Marks & Spencer after the Second World War. They perceived that the women who had freedom and independence away from home in the services or doing war work were not going to come back and sit at home of an evening sewing and dressmaking as they or their elder sisters had done before the war. They also saw that many of these women would want to be out working and would have more money to spend on clothes. Another thing they anticipated was that, as a result of wearing uniform or garments which because of the exigencies of rationing were of a classless design and cut, women of modest means had become accustomed to dressing in the same way as more well-to-do women – and *vice versa*. This, therefore, thought Simon and Israel, was a time for the democratization of women's clothing. Accordingly they introduced a range of inexpensive, modern, easy-to-wear women's clothing, which, because there was not too large a variety of designs, could be manufactured and marketed at relatively low prices. Their perception of social and economic changes allied to their ability to adjust to and profit from them enabled Marks & Spencer to make another leap forward.

The story of my friend Bob Anderson and Arco (Atlantic Richfield Oil Company) one of the biggest oil companies in America, is an interesting example of how expertise, perception and good luck combined to produce spectacular success.

Bob had made up his mind as a teenager to go into the oil business because he was so struck by the personality and life-style of the oil men who came to visit his father in his Chicago bank, all of whom were very much outdoor men keen on fishing and shooting. Bob was much more interested in living the outdoor life than in getting rich out of oil. So, having gained a geology degree at Chicago University, at the age of twenty-two, he borrowed some money from his father to buy a third share in a sleepy, small and none too bright-looking oil refinery in the wilds of New Mexico. He was to act as manager of this somewhat dilapidated little refinery, employing thirty-five men, with the object of getting some experience. This he proceeded to do with evident success, so much so that he was soon able to buy out his less efficient partner.

A while later Bob learned that not far away was a United States Army flying field, which was coming into much greater use as a result of America's entry into the Second World War. The air field, flying Boeings, required high octane fuel – 91 octane aviation gas. Bob's modest plant had never produced anything with so high an octane rating and his assistant manager warned him that, if he tried to use his existing equipment to produce 91 octane fuel, he would probably blow up the whole plant. Nothing deterred, Bob got out his college textbooks and mastered the theory. He then told everybody to clear out of the plant whilst he personally put his theory into practice. He got the high octane content and, to the surprise of his staff, the machinery did not explode. He took his fuel to the airfield, signed a contract, bought some trucks, and never looked back. He bought another refinery, then another, then went into the exploration of oil and gas resources, negotiated mergers and takeovers, and the result, thirty years later was Arco, one of the foremost oil companies, owning the second largest oil field in the world on the North slope bordering the Arctic Ocean.

Another remarkable story is that of Akio Morita, co-founder of Sony. After the Second World War young Morita joined forces with his friend and colleague Masaru Ibuka, who, like him, had a considerable knowledge of and interest in telecommunications. They pooled their financial resources, a little over £100, and set up a company called Tokyo Tsushin Kogyo, the Tokyo Telecommunication Engineering Company. Young Morita continued to teach part time at the Tokyo Institute of Technology whilst they set themselves up in a dilapidated shack on Tokyo Bay, the roof of which was so full of holes made by American bombs that, when it rained, they had to continue working under umbrellas.

Their first task was to decide what to make. It was suggested to them that they manufacture radio receivers, but they decided against this, believing that in no time at all the big companies would recover from the effects of the war and soon dominate the market. This negative decision was, in time, to prove crucial. Meanwhile, they decided to produce something that would be entirely new in Japan, a wire recorder. This turned out not to be a good idea; so they turned their attention to producing a tape recorder, but they did not know how to produce the all-important part of the equipment, the recording *tape*.

I do not know which is the more extraordinary, that they had the temerity to produce a recorder without knowing how to produce a tape or that, finding themselves with a recorder and no tape, with no inhibitions they set about producing the tape. They had no base material. They had no plastic. What they did have was some cellophane. They decided to slice the cellophane into long strips a quarter inch wide and then try coating them with various materials in turn to see if any of them worked, and, if so, which did best. However, they soon found that cellophane did not stand up to passage through the recording mechanism. After trying various expedients, they had a breakthrough. They found a paper of suitable quality, cut enough of it to make up a small reel, laid the strip out on the floor of their shack and coated it with a magnetic material. For this purpose they chose oxalic ferrite, which they heated to the right temperature in a frying-pan, mixing in some Japanese lacquer, and painted it on the paper strip by hand with fine paint brushes normally used for calligraphy.

They swiftly improved the process and by 1950 they had a really serviceable tape recorder. The irony is that they could not sell it. In those days hardly anyone in Japan had heard of a tape recorder and nobody saw any point in buying one. The founders of Sony, of all people, had to learn that it is not enough to have a good product or even a brilliant one – you have to sell it, which means making people see the point of possessing it.

It still strikes me as barely credible that the founders of Sony had to tell the world that a tape recorder was a good thing. This is not the only lesson I have learned from Mr Morita's fascinating book *Made in Japan*; elsewhere in this book I shall make other references to it and particularly to their enlightened philosophy of management and profound, creative concern for human relations in industry.

What do the origins of the various enterprises described above have in common? Several things, including ambition in one sense or another, though not simply to be rich. My two grandfathers were ambitious primarily to get away from persecution and live as free men. They were prepared to work hard and later become wealthy. I know many men who have become very wealthy; they all started out determined to work hard obviously wanting to make enough money to have a decent standard of living, but I doubt they would have been put off their chosen course by being told they would not end up wealthy.

The first thing an entrepreneur must have to start a business is vision; the second is determination. Those who started with nothing or very little were ready to get up and go, half way across a continent, if necessary half way across the world. They were ready to work hard and play little. Those who became most successful enjoyed their work. They were ready to learn, and take trouble in learning. Most got on well with people; they understood their customers, treated them well, and treated their employees well too. They could organize.

Once their businesses were under way, then I think their initial successes showed the crucial importance of *perception*. They perceived a market where there was unfulfilled demand or where they succeeded in meeting a demand with better quality and/or better value goods or services.

I have emphasised the importance of perception; but perception must be backed up by research. In that excellent regular feature in *The Times* entitled 'Your Own Business' I read recently about a young businesswoman by the name of Mary Balfour, who two years ago set up a new agency for introducing people to one another. There are more than a thousand of these agencies in existence; many have failed in the past. It is a high-risk area into which to pitch one's enterprise. What made Ms Balfour enter it? According to *The Times*, 'I have always been fascinated by human relationships and bringing people together. ... Even before I set the business up, I had about fifteen marriages to my credit, as a result of people I had introduced on a non-professional basis.' But, she added, 'It was obvious from the start that, if I was going to make a success of things, I'd have to identify a gap in the market.'

That is important – very important – *identify a gap in the market*. Before she took the plunge, she spent twelve months researching the field, in her own words 'looking for a gap in an overcrowded market'. Mary Balfour took a good look at what other agencies had to offer. As a result, she decided the way for her to go was to provide an up-market, personalized introduction for well-off, well-educated young to middle-aged professional people who, because of the type of work they were doing, were not likely to meet or form relationships with members of the opposite sex in the usual way.

She set up the agency with £20,000 from her bank, her friends and some investors, and took advice from the Government's Small Firms Advisory Service. She looks like being very successful. Why? So far as I can see because she was interested in and cared about people, and saw a gap in the market where that interest of hers could be beneficially applied all round, and had the wit to avail herself of free advice about it.

In the *Observer* of 16 October 1988 I saw a headline 'Room at the Top' and because, as my reader will by now know, it is a theme which interests me, I read the article and learned about Angela Heylin, the chairman of Charles Barker Public Relations. She was profiled because she had just received an award for her contribution to the industry. She is now a Fellow of the Institute of Public Relations.

Hers really is a story of room at the top. After taking her A-levels, she decided to train as a secretary. At the end of her training she was told that, if she worked hard for the next five or six years as a shorthand typist, she could then expect to become a qualified private secretary. It would be nice to be able to record something like 'From that moment Angela Heylin never looked back,' but life, even for those bound for the top, is not always like that. When she decided to cease being a secretary and, as she put it, 'crossed to the other side of the desk', she had to make a fresh effort. 'I trudged round the agencies in search of a job.' When she found one which seemed worthwhile, she realized she would have to start at a smaller salary than she had been earning as a secretary and work longer hours, indeed indeterminate hours, since it was clear to her that to hold down the job she would have to work after hours at home. But none of this deterred her; having spotted her personal gap in the market, she was determined to make the most of it and she has no regrets.

Perception is all important. However, it is not always just perception of a market or even of one's own potential that brings great rewards. Success may come, for example, from perception of an alternative method of production, of costs that can be saved or of a more attractive presentation. The man who saw the possibilities of the sale of mustard realized that, though the amount of mustard which a customer would actually consume with his beef or his bacon would be small, the amount he would put on his plate would be very large, and that the profit would come not from what was swallowed but from what was left.

The Showering family made fine cider at good profit in Somerset, but, when they produced a high-quality sparkling drink from pears packaged cleverly in a bottle resembling champagne and called it Babycham, they became millionaires.

While still an up-and-coming young tycoon my friend Arnold Weinstock, walking around a radio-manufacturing plant, paused to chat with a man putting brass screws into the backs of radio sets to keep them firmly in place. Arnold asked if the backs being fitted needed to be so thick, and was told that they need not. He thereupon decided that the backs should be thinner. From that time on much shorter screws were used and the company saved itself large sums hitherto spent on brass screws.

My favourite story about perspicacity paying off is one which many people have heard and may well be apocryphal. One day the manufacturers of a famous matchstick received a letter from somebody they had never heard of saying, in effect, 'I could save you a considerable sum of money. If you would let me have half

what you save, I will come and see you and tell you what to do.'
The manufacturers invited him to come along. When he arrived,
he said to them, 'At the moment, you have a strip of sandpaper
to ignite the match on both edges of the matchbox. One will
suffice.' He was well rewarded. This may not be a true story, but
it illustrates a valuable point.

Perception can apply to many other areas of business, to packaging, for example, of slogans or names. The name 'Babycham',
with its suggestions of champagne, sold a great deal of cider. I
wonder how many barrels of stout were sold when somebody
perceived the effect of the phrase 'Guinness is good for you.' This
is where the skill, the art, under the aegis of an advertising agency
often asserts itself. But for continued success a good name or
slogan is not enough; it is essential that the product or service is
well made/efficient and desirable, and represents good value.

Fortunes have been made by the early perception of environmental change or by the anticipation of the uses of new man-
made raw materials or sources of energy. Ecological change and
human reaction to it can bring fresh opportunities to those who
spot them in time, and swift failure to those who do not detect
changes in taste and opinion.

When I look at the acorns which have grown into oaks I am
struck by the number which have done so on account of a
partnership, not necessarily a formal partnership, but often as the
result of an informal one, a friendship, perhaps, or the relationship
between husband and wife. Sometimes it is a case of the other
person bringing valuable knowledge and experience into the
partnership; sometimes of bringing little or no technical knowledge, but vital moral support or just human company; perhaps
all of these. It is very important for the budding entrepreneur,
however gifted, self-confident and individualistic, however much
of a loner, to have somebody to talk to, and I think sometimes

that the more egocentric the entrepreneur the more important it is for him to have somebody he can confide in, whether it is his wife, a chum or his bank manager. The best example of this that I know of was the relationship between Simon Marks and my father.

Before the First World War, Simon as a young man had taken over Marks & Spencer upon the early death of his father. Marks & Spencer was a small but growing business. In the mid-1920s Marks & Spencer was making good progress, its headquarters by then in London, to where Simon had moved from Manchester. My father, Simon's close friend and brother-in-law, was running his father's business in Manchester. He was a director of Marks & Spencer, and regularly went down to London for board meetings, staying with Simon. There came a period when Simon was embarking on a considerable expansion, which some of his board did not favour. My father could see that Simon was unhappy, so one evening he asked him what the matter was. Simon blurted out, 'I've nobody to talk to, I'm surrounded by a lot of bloody idiots.' A few weeks later my father left Manchester and moved into Simon's office, each at his own desk; this was in 1926 and it was the beginning of a remarkable partnership, to which two very different men with various gifts contributed. My father appreciated the importance of good human relations at work, as did Simon; Father was open and easy to talk to. Simon had vision and leadership qualities; he knew into what type of retail business he wanted Marks & Spencer to develop, a chain of fine stores selling a limited range of high quality goods, mainly in clothing and then later foodstuffs. Father had considerable experience of textiles and fabrics, both of which proved most valuable in Marks & Spencer's clothing development, as did several other of his qualifications, but in the beginning his greatest contribution to the partnership was that he was somebody for Simon to talk to.

This relationship was in contrast to the original Marks & Spencer partnership. Michael Marks wanted to expand his small but growing business in the 1890s. He needed somebody who would mind the office, while he was out looking for sites for his little bazaar shops and market stalls, and purchasing goods. He wanted someone to deal with the reception and payment of the goods, to run the office and do the administrative work. So he invited Tom Spencer, the cashier in the office of Isaac Dewhirst, the Leeds merchant who lent Michael the fiver that started him off, to join him. In Dewhirst's records for July 1895 it is noted: 'Tom Spencer came to tell me that he proposed to give three months notice and join Michael Marks'. Then Isaac Dewhirst reported in September: 'Spencer left today to join Michael Marks.' Michael had understanding and drive. Tom was not a leader, but he contributed vital expertise which Michael needed at the time.

With the possible need for partnership goes the need for a sufficiently able staff. Without this, the incipient business may soon collapse as a result of the founder taking on too much too soon. With few adequately trained staff it is critically important for a new or expanding business not to go too fast. (I shall expand on this point later.)

If you are thinking of starting a new business or shifting one already in existence into a higher gear, there is one major factor you should consider. Can you, perhaps with the aid of your partners, command enough capital to keep you going in the early period in which your judgement of demand is on trial? You may begin to make a good sale on the first day or in the first week, but can you keep going long enough if things are sticky to give your products or your service a fair chance to become established in the market? Market research is now a sophisticated technique, but, however much it can tell you about how many people *might* buy what you have to offer, it can never *make* people buy what you have to sell. Market research, therefore, combined with the advice of Government agencies and of a bank manager, can give you a good idea what you will require for your launch in terms of cash and credit. But nothing you will be told can be regarded as guarantees which expectant and grateful customers have enthusiastically endorsed.

Another key ingredient for success in a new or expanding business is commitment.

I have mentioned the need for perception, research, suitable support (perhaps partnership) and capital. I have also mentioned hard work, ambition and the ability to work well with other people. The three latter are extremely important, but you must also be prepared, certainly in the early days and maybe for some years, to commit yourself to your business to a degree which might be described as obsessive. In the early days of a new business you have to be on deck all the time, and your wife/girl-friend or your husband/boyfriend will have to face it. One of the motives which will attract new customers to you is their assumption that, since you are new and relatively inexpensive, you are available at virtually all times. If they find your telephone or answering machine is telling them 'not here at the moment', they may not call back.

From the beginning, whether you are the most recently recruited employee, a junior executive or presiding over the fortunes of your own new business, however small, you are part of the image of the business and responsible for that part.

Many business people, it seems to me from what I have seen and heard, are not aware of the company image which can be created by the telephone, and that is true for individuals also. One of the hallmarks of a well-organized and attractive business, large or small, is the impression created by the response of its staff to a telephone call. When a customer, a contact or a newspaper reporter, etc., telephones your number, how does the person who answers sound? Does he immediately announce the name of the firm or, if it is your personal secretary speaking, give your personal name in a brisk but friendly, courteous and helpful way? Or does he only say, 'Hello', and then wait for the caller to say something else? Does he answer the telephone while in the middle of a conversation with somebody sitting nearby? Has he taken your call while in the middle of a giggle about something? – a frequent and maddening professional discourtesy. Does the person representing you, your department or your firm sound interested, efficient and polite, or does he sound bored or resentful at being disturbed?

I continue to be amazed by the number of businesses whose telephonic images leave much to be desired. Whether you are a big businessman or a small one, and particularly if you are a recent starter or the head of a department with its own telephone exchange, ring your number from time to time from outside and see how your first line of ambassadors are representing you.

Most of the shortcomings on the telephone front in a business result from the fact that the telephonists, whether they are two or twenty in number, are shut away from the rest of the staff and are treated not as vital members of the total operation, but as backroom operators of the most inferior and unimportant kind, with hardly anybody even knowing their names – 'Oh, leave a message with the telephone boy/girl.' A good executive will see to it that his telephonists are chosen with care, are trained in an office style which is acceptable to them, and made to feel that they are individuals with an up-front responsibility for the initial good image of the company. The executive should make sure that he visits them from time to time and that his own telephone contacts with them are friendly and respectful. As for secretaries, he is an unfortunate executive, whether junior or chairman of whom colleagues or friends say behind his back, 'His secretary's a bit of a bitch.'

You should also consider your own behaviour on the telephone and to the telephone operator. It does not matter who you are or how important you are in the business, correct treatment of telephone operators is essential – they are an important asset. I regularly visit the Marks & Spencer telephone exchange to thank them for their good work.

To some extent the commitment required to start or maintain a responsible business excludes many non-business activities and largely dominates the way you spend your life even after you have become successful. Simon Marks enjoyed playing tennis, being on a yacht, going to the races and collecting paintings; he enjoyed the society of stimulating and congenial people; he gave great support to public works. My father loved music, collected pictures, enjoyed country pursuits and gardening, bred high-class cattle and raised rare orchids. Their wives, children and grandchildren generally shared in these interests and pursuits, but all through the weekends, many of which Simon and Father spent together, their business interests or, as they might have said, their business responsibilities, came up for discussion frequently. Business discussions did not cease when they left the office at 5.30 p.m. or from Friday afternoon till Monday morning.

A painter can, if he wishes, put down his brush and turn his back on his canvas for a day, a week or a month before he returns to it. A writer, unless he is a day-to-day journalist, can close the manuscript of his new opus with no intention of opening it again until he feels in the mood to do so. The musician, if he feels inspiration has left him or wishes to give his mind to something else, can pause in the composition of a masterpiece; Wagner, for instance, broke off the composition of the *Ring* for seven years and then resumed the creation of that epic cycle. But the business-man, the entrepreneur, the challenger in the marketplace and particularly the new entrant in the early days of his debut in business must be ready initially to give virtually his whole waking time to his chosen field.

A first business venture is often a risky undertaking personally as well as professionally for a young person newly married, especially if there are young children to be looked after: even after he and his business have achieved success, if he wants to develop further, he will have to keep his nose to the grindstone. The demands of a successful business take up the majority of the entrepreneur's time, man or woman, and consume a great deal of that person's energy. This is how it should be, since business, like our creative arts, are the white corpuscles of the lifeblood of our society. The vast majority of men and women starting up a business or developing further an already successful one enjoy their work – and the great majority do so despite the problems which often face them at home.

So, given perception, ambition, the capacity for hard work, personal and professional support, a reasonable amount of capital and sound advice, success in business also requires much con-centration and the readiness to work long hours. If only in this respect, it might be said that successful businessmen are born but not often made.

If you have decided that you are ready and willing to take the risk of starting your own business you still have to make various decisions. The main question you have to answer is what requi-sites for your business you can provide yourself and what you may have to recruit other people for.

(We assume at this stage that, if you are going into business to market a particular product or service, you have made as sure as you possibly can through your own observation and thorough market research that there is a market for it. We assume, too, that you have satisfactorily answered the following questions. If no one has supplied such a product/service before, is this because there is no demand for it? If it has been on the market before, was its lack of success due to the fact that it was not presented properly?)

The question of what you can personally provide for the business and what expertise you need to recruit arises from the fact that business success depends on three things: running the business; selling the product; expertise in the production of goods. There are some remarkable people who are good at all three aspects and you may be one of them, but you would be unwise to take all three functions on yourself unless you can do so without incurring too much financial embarrassment if things go wrong and the results do not meet your expectations.

The most straightforward task – not the same as being the easiest, it may be very arduous especially in the early stages – is that of the person in charge of production. Whether he is producing something like a new food or a service like a travel agency, his job begins and ends with producing efficiently something of competitive quality which can be sold at competitive prices.

The product being the key factor, the producer, if he has good judgement, can recruit the administration and marketing forces he needs. Many producers, however, have proved incapable of doing so and the business has consequently failed.

Whereas the production man's expertise lies in his technical knowledge and how to apply it, the salesman depends as much on his personality as on his knowledge of the market and the products competing in it. Some salesmen have so succeeded in their business careers that they have ended up as chairmen or chief executives of substantial corporations, sometimes because a company has had to face the fact that, as well as producing high-quality goods, it has to sell them in very large quantities in order to survive, and the salesman's talent has been crucial in persuading the public to do so. But, however great a salesman's talent is, unless the product or service represents good value and quality, the salesman will not be successful for long.

The main thing for *you* to decide is what your gifts are, what you are best at. Do not try to do everything yourself, but capitalize your qualifications and recruit others to do the rest.

If you are going to set up your own business, do not hesitate to take advice before you start. You can get it from many sources, ranging from banks to the small firms division of the Department of Trade and Industry in London. Bear in mind, too, the Rural Development Commission (into which the Council for Small Industries in Rural Areas was merged in 1988) with its headquarters in London, and also the possibility of consulting your Local Authority. Not only will you receive valuable advice but also possibly financial assistance as well from the Enterprise Allowance scheme, for example, or from the Business Expansion scheme. Your bank will give you, if not all the information you require, at least the names of those who can help.

If you are starting a business, you will probably decide to do one of four things: open up as a sole trader (which does not mean that you cannot employ people); set up a partnership; establish a limited company; or buy a business which already exists. You must take advice about which of these will suit you best and, when you have chosen, take advice about how to begin to operate.

Remember that before you can start to trade there are legal requirements for all these forms of business. Even if you go for the simplest and operate as a sole trader, you must immediately begin doing three things: keep books and records for tax purposes, and have them up-to-date for the tax inspector to look at if he decides to call; register for VAT if your sales are going to be on a level above the current limit – consult the local VAT office; and, if you are going to be an employer, you will have to submit PAYE returns – consult the local branch of the Department of Social Security.

Unless you will have enough time and are able to do the job yourself, you will need a full-time or part-time accountant.

Over the last few decades many more businesses than in the past have been run by accountants. Some accountants make good administrators, and some good administrators make good chief executives. One should not generalize too freely, but it is part of an accountant's professional function to be cautious, meticulous, critical and analytical. He is there not to advise taking risks but rather to urge and advise you how to avoid them. Though there are exceptions to the rule, accountants therefore do not generally make the best principals and, though they may render great, even crucial, service in the early days of a small business, they may not be suitable to lead and energize it.

The key factor in building up a successful business, however, is to develop a successful team. Even a small business needs to exploit a variety of gifts in order to succeed. The role of the leader is to select the right men and women, and inspire and direct them to work as a team.

three

HOW TO GET ON
IN BUSINESS

In this section I offer my views on how people starting their
career should behave if they want to get on in business and
at the same time enjoy it to the full. Some readers may regard
these remarks so obviously a matter of common sense as to be
unnecessary. All I can say in answer is: it is often the simplest
wisdom which is the most difficult to find, and common sense is
not commonly distributed.

Unless your career choice and first job in a company are
influenced in advance – perhaps by a relative or family friend
suggesting you get a job in the company he is working for – you
will have to make a choice. If so, it is worth while investigating
carefully the options as to what kind and size of company you
would like to work for. Whatever research and enquiry you
undertake on your own, I would strongly recommend you to
have a look at the *The 100 Best Companies to Work For in the U.K.*
by Bob Reynolds with foreword by Sir John Harvey-Jones and
published by Fontana. I recommend it not because several of the
firms I most admire are included, and not because Marks &
Spencer receives a particularly complimentary mention, but
because, as well as telling the reader a good deal about these
hundred firms, the book should open many a young person's
eyes to the numerous ways in which even successful firms differ
not only in size, job prospects, pay and location, but also in terms

of ambience, atmosphere and ethos.

An intelligent young man or woman reading this book would, I think, start to ask useful questions not only about what kind of company they would like to work for but also about themselves. You cannot make up your mind about what you want to do without thinking a bit about what you are.

Before beginning his book, Bob Reynolds drew up a list of the criteria on which he and his research team would base their enquiries. These were: pay, benefits, promotion, training, equal opportunities, environment, ambience and communications. He had his eye open on such questions as how women are treated, and which companies are best for graduates, which for non-graduates. I was struck by the variation in size of his view of the top one hundred. For example, among the big employers are BP – 128,000 in seventy countries; ICI – 127,800, more than half outside the UK; Bass – 80,194 in the UK; and British Aerospace – 75,000 in several locations around the South-East of Britain. Among the small ones are: Compaq, the rapidly expanding computer company – 200 employees; Body Shop – 351; and Johnson's Wax – 600.

One of the book's most important messages for a young person thinking of going into business is the wide variety displayed by this relatively small sample of firms. Some are highly dynamic and the internal atmosphere reflects this; others are more easy going. Some are tough negotiators; others are more relaxed. Some favour considerable perks; others pay high salaries with few or no perks, while pension schemes vary. Several of these companies are located in highly desirable environments, for instance Robertson Research is in a mansion just behind the North Wales seaside resort of Llandudno; others are in central London. Some make very high profits, while some do not. But in the eyes of Bob Reynolds all qualify for membership of the top 100 companies, and the reasons he gives for their inclusion are well worth reading.

Anybody who wants to succeed in business should begin his first day with the belief that there is nothing but the limits of his own capacity that can prevent him getting to the very top. Every private soldier carries a marshal's baton in his knapsack Napoleon is supposed to have said; and if he did not in fact say it, he certainly would have said something like it if he had started his career where I did in the basement of the Marks & Spencer store in Hammersmith, London.

From the very start, even before your first day in business, there are four elementary, but outstanding, factors which will affect your career: appearance, behaviour, personality, and the ability to express yourself clearly and simply.

Most people can do little to change their personality, but everybody can do something about the other three. Perhaps because these things are so elementary many intelligent people neglect them until long after they should have been benefiting from their application.

A wealthy dentist friend of mine at the very top of his profession has said to me more than once: 'Marcus, most of my fees come from my older patients who are paying me for treatment which would have been unnecessary if twenty years ago they had started to do a few simple things to their teeth and gums which I told them to do free. Why didn't they do them? Probably because what I told them to do was so simple, obvious common sense. Clean your teeth properly night and morning, and massage your gums for a minute or so. But they didn't do it. Now they pay me large fees for repairing the damage they could perfectly well have prevented for themselves.'

Any discussion about how to get on in business should begin with how one gets into business in the first place and, since it may well be that you will get your first job through an interview, I offer some thoughts on how to come through it successfully. The key points about an interview for your first job will apply equally to any interviews later on in life: in some large organizations even very senior executives have to appear before internal boards before they are promoted.

Above all comes the desirability of being able to express yourself clearly and simply. You do not need to go to university or college to be able to do so. Some people are born with this ability; those who are not can benefit from practice and self-criticism. Go into any pub and you will hear people expressing themselves very clearly and simply about a whole range of topics from last Saturday's football match to a current Government crisis. To improve your own ability to express yourself, listen to other people critically, and listen to yourself critically as well. The ability to talk efficiently can be cultivated, and you should practice it. You do not have to strain to make yourself into an orator, simply aim to make yourself articulate, that will be quite enough, and you will be able to do so without much stress.

For many people the most important interview is the first. Let us suppose you are trying to get a job either with the first firm at which you have set your cap or having spent the first few years of your working life with another. What should you bear in mind, and what should you do?

1. Try to impress them before they see you. Reply to their advertisement or make your application to them in a simple, clear, direct manner. If you can possibly do this in type-written form, you should. Access to typewriters today is not difficult. Once you know you are going to be interviewed, write to confirm where and when the interview will take place, and ask them to send you a copy of any publication giving the latest information available about the company. Show an interest in the company as well as in the job you are applying for; the two things are, after all, part of the same whole. You may already know quite a lot about the business from

talking with friends and acquaintances, reading the newspapers and from any inquiries you have been able to make, but it does no harm to get a set of answers from the company in their own words and on their own terms. Also, if you ask for the information, it will show that you are a serious, methodical, responsible applicant for the job.

Ask politely if you can be told who will interview you and what he or she does in the company. If you have already been given this information, do not ask for it again. Indeed, do not risk irritating busy people by asking for information contained in the appointments advertisement and do not ask for information which your interviewers know you could easily have acquired elsewhere if you were really interested in joining them.

2. Experienced interviewers argue about the time it takes to assess an interviewee. Some say that they arrive at a tentative view as soon as the candidate comes into the room, others within the first minute, others that it takes longer. Take no chances with *your* first interview or your second, or your third: be on time; be as neatly dressed as you know how; and come into the room smiling, not grinning, but looking as though you are going to enjoy the experience of meeting new and interesting people whether or not you get the job. It may be that by the time you get into the room you will have been told the name of the interviewer or the chairman of the inter-viewing board. If he says, 'Good morning, Mr Smith,' to you, respond with 'Good morning, Mr Jones.'

3. The probability is that the interviewer and/or his col-leagues will have all the documents they need before them on the table, some of them submitted by you – your curriculum vitae, for example – but it does no

harm to take your own little dossier. If you do, be sure you have mastered it, so that if you want to refer to anything in it you can do so without the slightest waste of time and without the risk of spilling it over the floor.

At the end of such an interview the interviewer(s) may ask if there is anything else you would like to know about the job you have applied for. It will do no harm if you produce a note of one or two questions you have prepared in advance, to which you might feel like adding one or more questions which arise as a result of what has come up in the interview.

The chances are that you will have a fair idea of the starting salary before the interview takes place, possibly from reading the job advertisement or you may have been able to make a deduction about it in the light of your own knowledge and experience of the going rates. In any case, you should bear in mind that potential employers are much more impressed by applicants who ask what are their prospects for advancement within the company than by those who want to know at once what they are likely to be paid. Throughout an interview, to maximise his success, the interviewee must strike a balance between being interviewed and interviewing.

By chance, as I was working on this section of the book, a friend who is head of a medium sized company came to lunch. We were discussing the development of his modest but successful and growing business. He told me that that very morning he had interviewed a young man in his early twenties who came with relatively good references; he said the major subject the interviewee wanted to know about was what his pension would be and how it would be funded. My friend could not believe his ears. The young man did not get the job.

Once you are in the firm you must regard yourself as continually and unremittingly on parade. It may not be true to say that somebody is always looking at you, but it is certainly true to say that always somebody might be. Promotion is often the result of being in the right place at the right time. The trouble is that we often do not know where or when this will be – luck enters into it as well as good appearance and ability. Best assume that the right place and the right time are here and now, wherever you are and whatever the hour. One of my favourite sayings is: 'God sends the winds; we must prepare the sails.' Always be ready and shipshape to seize your chance if it comes. Let me give you an example.

It was the rule of Marks & Spencer that all management recruits, other than technologists and specialists, who hope to make a career in head office have to spend their first two years working in the stores. This rule so far as I am personally concerned was only broken once some thirty-five years ago, when one Saturday morning I visited the store in Oxford. As we left the food department to look at other parts of the store, the manager, Mr Gibson, said, 'If Mr Rayner didn't seem to know much about the food department, you must make allowances – he's only been in it a week. He's a new recruit, he only joined us a few months ago.' In fact I had been most impressed with Mr Rayner's knowledge and suggestions, and went back to talk to him. I found out that he had studied at Selwyn College, Cambridge, with a view to taking holy orders, but had decided it was not for him. He had then set up in a retail fancy goods business in his home town of Norwich, but, having decided there was insufficient scope, he joined Marks & Spencer.

On the following Monday morning at head office I went to the director of personnel, Norman Laski, and to Cedric Woolf, the head of store operations. I said I would like Derek Rayner brought into the food group. They refused: he had not spent his two years in the stores. 'Well, it's a very good rule, but good rules are made to be broken on occasion and this is just such an occasion,' I replied. They still did not agree, but I insisted. They asked if I was agreeable to leaving Derek Rayner in Oxford to help in the store over the holiday period – it was then June; after he had had his own holidays, he could come into head office, probably at the end of October. I said, 'Yes,' but they were annoyed with my seeming to put a pistol at their heads.

A few weeks later, on a visit to the Watford store, I saw an apparently familiar figure on the first floor. It was Derek Rayner. I asked him what he was doing. He said he had been transferred to Watford shortly after my visit to Oxford. The day was again a Saturday; on the following Monday in head office I played merry hell and said that, unless Derek Rayner was in head office by the following Monday, I would take up the matter with the chairman. Derek was in by the following Monday. That young man is now Lord Rayner, chairman and chief executive of Marks & Spencer.

I have already referred to Bob Anderson. I much enjoy his story of how his father, Hugo, starting as a fourteen-year-old messenger boy, rose to become executive vice president of the First National Bank of Chicago, one of the greatest banks in the United States. Hugo was under-sized for his age, but his personality and energy were noted by many of his seniors at the bank.

One morning young Hugo, by this time aged sixteen, was waiting to be given some errands in the room of the president of the bank, James B. Forgan. Also present was Forgan's assistant, August Blum. Forgan asked Blum if he could produce a recent report on the affairs of a bank in St Louis; a big deal could be brought off if Blum could produce the report immediately. Blum could not do so, and went back to his own office mortified and worried. Young Hugo followed him there and said: 'There's an out-of-town newspaper stand across the street. There'll be St

Louis newspapers there, and the report could be in one of them.'
Blum told him to go and look. Young Hugo found the report.
Blum was so delighted that he took Hugo and the newspaper to
Forgan's office. 'What we couldn't think of, this boy did,' he told
Forgan. From that day on Hugo Anderson made his way up in
the bank with steadiness and speed, ending his career as one of
the most famous bankers in America.

Such luck, however, generally helps those who help
themselves. Once you work for a company you must identify
with the company you work for and feel that its interests are your
own. I was brought up to breathe and eat Marks & Spencer, and
my wife often complained to me that Marks & Spencer came first
in my life. Such commitment and dedication are vital if you want
to get to the top.

four

GOING TOO FAST

One of the most dangerous temptations an up-and-coming business entrepreneur may have to face is to go too far too fast. New businesses are the most likely to succumb, but well-established businesses, too, may expand into fresh areas too quickly with results that can lead to serious losses and which, if not dealt with in time, can be disastrous.

A successful business's rate of growth depends on having an adequate number of trained staff and capital to cope with the planned expansion. The demand for more goods or services may be there, adequate sources of supply may be available, but if you do not have both sufficient capital and a sufficient number of trained staff and, as a result, have to spread your resources too widely or too thinly, then the business may collapse. Another cause of failure is overestimating the demand and providing resources to meet a demand which is not there. On the other hand, there is no point undertaking to expand and distribute production when an adequate supply of human resources to tackle a real growth in demand is not available.

It is right to be ambitious, but it is important for whoever is in charge not to overestimate his or her capacity. It is very tempting, I believe, when one is young and ambitious, and has successfully started a new enterprise to misjudge the capacity of one's assets, particularly one's human assets, to take on more and more before one has sufficient experience personally and one's staff are adequately trained to cope with the expansion. I must re-emphasize that the main danger is to take on too much with too few adequately trained people, including oneself.

I am asked, 'Why do successful businessmen, hard-headed and practical, make such an elementary mistake as to go too far too fast? Creative, impulsive over-sanguine mortals, yes; gamblers, writers, actors, singers, yes; but why do materialistic and supposedly realistic entrepreneurs make such a mistake?' The answer is: because businessmen are often swayed by two emotions which cloud their judgement – ambition and competitiveness. Businessmen come a cropper because they want to show the world, especially their rivals, that they can do it better and more quickly than it has been done before; and often because they want to establish their ego in conflict with their peers. Businessmen are very human; if they were desiccated calculating machines, they would not be successful businessmen. Another important reason why they may come a cropper is that the man or woman in charge sometimes thinks they have more experience than in fact they have.

No matter what our walk of life, all success is heady, especially when it comes to us when we are young and even more so if it comes to us suddenly. For many of us one swallow *does* make a summer. 'The customers are beating on the door!' More goods are needed. 'Let's cash in on this.' More production at once. Bring more plant into production. Take on more staff, hire more workers. Obtain more credit from the bank – interest rates are high, but the way things are going we can afford it. Then, suddenly (or perhaps gradually), the demand falls away.

There are a number of reasons for a fall in demand for a product or service. Overall demand may be constant, but other people may have entered the market and competition increases. Problems arise which will be accentuated by the increased competition, by diminishing demand or by falling supplies. Sometimes demand diminishes or even ceases because of external factors over which the most farsighted businessman has little or no control. This is why it is imperative to do the utmost possible in research, testing and forecasting before embarking on a long-term commitment.

Marks & Spencer made just such an error of judgement some years ago when we leased a number of stores in western Canada. We saw that there was wealth in the area, earned mainly by those working in a booming oil industry. Those who worked on the oil rigs were the highest paid group in the area, many earning a minimum of $1,000 a week and I am talking of over ten years ago. Many of the oil rigs were some distance away from the nearest town, so the oil workers worked three weeks on and one week off in the nearest town. They spent money during their week off as if there were no tomorrow. Our stores flourished.

Then came a day when the price of oil collapsed and the oil industry suddenly changed dramatically. Most oil rigs closed down and the oil workers left the area to find work elsewhere. Sales were badly hit and, from being profitable, our stores began to lose money. It had been our practice in the United Kingdom, wherever possible, to own property, but in the Canadian shopping malls one had to lease properties – generally owners insisted on a long lease – rents were high, and the cost of closing a store and getting rid of the lease was even higher. Another problem was delivery distances. The road distance in the UK between our two stores which are furthest apart, Inverness and Falmouth, is 700 miles; in Canada between St John's, Newfoundland, and Vancouver it is 5,000 miles. Such great distances create delivery problems, particularly for food. We had not taken this into account.

Such considerations, readers may think, are so obvious that they could not possibly escape the attention of the average businessman. I can assure you that many large, sophisticated firms have come a cropper when they decided to go into business outside the country where they made a successful start, though it has to be said that others, too, have done the same in their own home country when they have neglected the golden rule of not going too fast too soon.

Another reason why the successful young entrepreneur should not go too fast in his early development is that he must learn how to anticipate and deal with changes in the market. If one is in the clothing business, for instance, one has to try to anticipate both changes in style or fashionable colours and also the damage which can be done by prolonged unseasonable weather. Sales of summer clothing will be much less if the weather is cold and wet, as will the sales of ice-cream. Equally, sales of cold weather lines in the autumn and winter will be affected if the weather is unseasonably warm. You have to make allowances if you are in such a business, particularly during your initial development phase. Failures and setbacks are not always due to human error but to factors difficult to foresee or control. As I said earlier, errors of judgement concerning public demand are different from miscalculations due to management misjudging what their team can do.

Why do intelligent and experienced businessmen, never mind beginners, make mistakes? Because, I think, the prospect of expansion, which means promotion and enhanced opportunity for ambitious, up-and-coming executives, is inclined to go to the head and temporarily vitiate prudence and sound judgement.

Firms which decide to expand quickly run the risk of unintentionally watering down the quality and value of their product and of their service to their customers, and, most important of all, the quality of their management. If a company expands too quickly it will not have enough trained managers at hand to exercise the quality control which has been essential to the success of their product in the market in the past. Firms which decide to expand their operations quickly may face the problem not only of quality but also of quantity. After having announced and promoted their new programme for the expanded distribution of their products or services, they may find they cannot deliver on the scale which they have promised and which the public (on the basis of their promises) expects. The problem of maintaining quality and quantity in expanding operations generally affects firms who rely on outside suppliers for some or all of their goods, but it can also affect firms which manufacture their own.

Significantly related to the problem of too rapid expansion is that of delegation. The first thing an expanding entrepreneur must do is recruit and develop a team, each one of whom, ideally, brings something useful to the business. Early on, too, may come the necessity for partnership as was evidenced in the situation of Michael Marks before he took on Tom Spencer.

The dangers of expanding too rapidly are at their worst in cases where firms do not stick to their forte, but are tempted into fields in which they have no expertise. Diversification can be successful, but many a company has got into trouble because it thought success in one enterprise qualified it for success in an enterprise of a very different nature.

Going too fast and not monitoring one's operation with seeing eyes or listening ears are a recipe for trouble.

One of the recent examples of going too fast is the history of the American firm Mrs Fields Inc. Creator of the soft cookie, the enterprising Debbi Fields rightly believed there was substantial demand for her product, so she and her husband started Mrs Fields Inc. Her product was first class and there was a great demand for it. They opened their first shop in 1977 and extended substantially. By 1983 the business had 140 stores with 1,500 employees in the USA, with 1983 sales totalling $26.2 million and pre-tax profits of $1.5 million. By 1987, with 4,500 employees, sales had increased to $102 million and pre-tax profits to $17.7 million, but the number of stores was being hugely increased. By 1988 there were over 550 stores worldwide, with outlets in Canada, Australia, Hong Kong, Japan and the UK. But by then it was clear that the business had expanded too fast. A number of new stores were far from profitable. The decision to close ninety stores during 1988 required a real estate write-down of $19.9 million, with the cost fully provided for in the 1988 accounts. The result of these closures was to reduce 1988 operating profit of $1.4 million to a net loss of $18.5 million in that year, against a net profit in 1987 of $17.7 million.

In an effort to diversify away from a single product strategy, the company purchased in 1987 a bakery business called La Petite Boulangerie from PepsiCo. This business enjoys advanced dough and baking technology, and once properly integrated into Mrs Fields Inc. will allow a wider range of goods for sale, bigger stores, and the possibility of better locations. But one of the main reasons for the collapse of profits in 1988 was the opening during the previous twenty-four months of too many new stores, including a number in overseas countries. It was beyond the capacity of the team to study thoroughly, amongst other things, the potential markets for the new stores and whether the catalogue was adequate. Also Mrs Fields Inc. could not manage efficiently so many stores spread worldwide. It is another example of the entrepreneur of a successful operation being tempted into developing too many units geographically too widely spread too quickly.

Since then the company has established a policy which should bring it back to profitability: to reduce expenses substantially by controlling costs, especially personnel; to test larger store concepts; to improve margin and some store sales on the basis of product diversification; and to conclude joint venture agreements and strategic alliances. I hope that as a result of the action the company's management has taken that Mrs Fields Inc. will make a good recovery. Both Mr and Mrs Fields themselves are very able people, but there is no doubt that the serious trouble they experienced was a result of expanding too fast.

I could give more examples and they could be drawn from many different fields of business, but what they have in common is the same lesson: do not go too far too fast.

five

GOOD HUMAN RELATIONS AT WORK

I wrote earlier that a successful business needs to be based on sound principles and that perhaps the most important of these was the implementation of a policy of good human relations at work for all concerned in and with the business. Of course such a principle will only be properly implemented if those at the top believe in it and set an example themselves; it cannot be done by the personnel department (often now called the human resources department) alone. Nowadays the majority of successful firms I know implement such a policy.

Good human relations involve a moral attitude: the chief executive has a duty to treat his employees as he would like to be treated himself, to do as he would be done by. He must treat everyone, no matter what their position, with respect, and all those in charge down the line must do the same for those whom they manage. In Marks & Spencer, for example, this goes for all who have any authority, for the supervisor of sales assistants and the foreman of the warehouse staff. I re-emphasise that it will only happen if those at the top set the example.

If one does not give credit for good work then employees will think or say 'Those bastards only criticise.' If, on the other hand, you do not criticise when it is justified and eventually, because of poor performance, have to dismiss someone, they are justified in their criticism of superiors when they say, 'No one told me what I was doing wrong.'

Good human relations at work pay off; they are of great importance if a business is to be efficiently run. An efficiently run business is generally profitable, and all should share in the profits, both the shareholders and those who work in the business. Efficiency leads to products and services of high quality and good value, and these in turn lead to increased sales and profit. This is so obvious that it is surprising how many business enterprises still fail to pay adequate attention to good human relations at work and have failed, to their cost, to implement such a policy. There are three main reasons for this failure: firstly senior management fails to understand its importance; secondly, they may understand it, but do not know how to set up the arrangements to get the policy implemented; and, thirdly, they may have made the arrangements, but do not know how to make them work.

Providing he or she appreciates the importance of good human relations, it is perhaps easier for a young person starting a business employing only a few people to implement such a policy. The leader sets the example and sees that it is implemented down the relatively short line. It is more difficult if the business is substantial and has not previously had such a policy, but in these days of increasing technology and computer use its implementation is more important than ever. Employees must not become mere cogs in a large machine. Unfortunately, some potential managers who have learned the skills necessary to deal with modern equipment do not possess or do not appreciate the skills required for dealing with people – and in the end it is people who make an operation work effectively and efficiently. The most modern sophisticated technological equipment still cannot work on its own; it needs some human guidance if it is to work well or sometimes even at all. In this era of rapid technological expansion the demand for good management is greater than ever.

An important factor in the profitable development of Marks & Spencer over the last sixty years has been the attention paid to implementing a policy of good human relations at work. Caring about employees began in Marks & Spencer from its earliest days. My grandfather, Michael Marks, was a caring employer. He did not invent caring – many men had been caring employers before him. Perhaps the most famous and commercially successful of them all was Robert Owen, the manager of mills in Lanarkshire, who proved what many Victorian mill masters would not believe: that you could pay your employees well, give them good working conditions, provide schools, housing and kitchens for them, even a village band, in general treating them as you would like to be treated yourself, and at the same time develop a fine industry which makes a good profit.

I do not suppose Michael Marks had ever heard of Robert Owen when he set up his stall in Leeds market, indeed I doubt whether he heard of him in the whole of his lifetime, but Michael had the same good instincts.

In 1984 my wife and I went up to Leeds, where the business had started one hundred years ago, to open a block of flats for the elderly which Marks & Spencer had financed as one of its centenary community projects. Lily and I were introduced to Mrs Stoker, then ninety years old. She had started work on my grandfather's market stall when she left school at the age of thirteen, in 1907. She lunched with us in the Leeds store dining-room. She was impressed by the staff dining-room and lounge, and remarked, 'We didn't have anything like this, but even in those days we had a little place over the stall where we could make hot drinks and have our sandwiches.' People working on the other market stalls, she said, did not have such facilities. When Michael Marks built his first head office in Derby Street, Manchester, at the beginning of the century, though he employed only a dozen or so people there, he provided them with their own dining-room and a kitchen where they could cook their food.

Simon Marks and my father carried on this tradition. They were spurred to do more by an incident in the early 1930s, when unemployment was at its height. Father and Simon on a visit to Kilburn store in London saw that one of the sales assistants behind the counter did not look well. They asked her if anything was wrong; she said no, she was all right. Father was not satisfied – he asked the manager to talk to her. The manager found out that the girl was not getting enough to eat; her father and brothers were unemployed and she was handing over her wages to help support them and the family, and there just was not enough to go round. 'No one who works for us must go hungry,' said Father. He and Simon immediately launched a scheme to provide all Marks & Spencer stores with facilities for a hot three-course meal in the middle of the day. Today such a facility is common-place. It was not sixty years ago.

Over the next twenty-five years they greatly widened and extended this programme, aided by a remarkable lady, Flora Solomon, who was in charge of what was then called welfare. I became very involved when I was head of personnel. During these years we introduced medical, dental, physiotherapy, hair-dressing and chiropody facilities. Many of these services cost the company a good deal, but they soon led to a more efficient and friendly staff, and better service to our customers. Each store has, for example, a visiting chiropodist. It is tiring for a sales assistant to be standing up for several hours at a go each day; it is a strain on the feet and makes demands on the nervous system. How can anyone be efficient and pleasant under such circumstances? Marks & Spencer do not want people who work for them to be under strain if they can help prevent it.

We introduced hairdressing for the staff because we found out that, when members of staff wanted their hair done, they would go during the lunch period and have no meal; hairdressing facilities ensured that staff could have their hair done and have time for lunch as well.

Some of these facilities are free; some are charged for at about a third or less of what the cost would be outside. They make for a more pleasant, healthy and comfortable staff, who are that much better at their work; they look after the customers better; and, if you can add good service, to goods of high quality and value, more are sold and, as a result, profits increase.

In dealing with various staff problems we found that, providing a decision was made quickly, the person concerned was generally satisfied. Hence we delegated responsibility to the local store manager and his team to deal with personnel problems, inevitable from time to time, and encourage them to act quickly and generously, but not precipitately. The local manager, in case of need, can make an immediate grant or loan of up to £100, or can extend sick pay beyond the normal time if there is a valid reason. This immediate response to individual needs is an important feature of our caring policy.

There are a number of cases with which local management are not allowed to deal. Such instances include long-term leave of absence due to illness, staff looking after elderly dependents, or staff needing loans because, through lack of budgetary understanding, they get themselves into financial difficulties. To deal with these problems a head office welfare committee was set up in 1933 and met weekly. (It now meets monthly as more is dealt with locally or regionally.) The welfare committee was asked to take a decision within a week; if that was not possible, they were requested to contact the individual concerned so that he or she knew that the problem was being looked at, again speed was of the essence. The members of the welfare committee are recruited from the senior members of our personnel, staff management and pensions departments. In recent years, because of the growth of the business, divisional welfare committees have been established, each covering about forty stores. Problems which cannot be decided at store or divisional level are referred to the monthly head office committee.

From time to time I hear people complaining that Marks & Spencer and other companies do these things not primarily for the welfare of their employees but ultimately to cut costs. Can reasonable people really believe that the two motives are incompatible? Life is not about this motive as opposed to that, this objective in distinction to that one. Though business is ultimately about the pursuit of profit, objectives and motivation in that pursuit are complex and sometimes conflicting. Reconciling and directing these motives and objectives is what enlightened management is about.

I sometimes think that opposition to this approach comes not from cynics but from the guilty. Cynicism and guilt are often bedfellows: X feels guilty that he is not doing what Y is doing, so he tries to rid himself of his guilt by impugning Y's motives. Occasionally opposition comes from the enemies of capitalism, who will not have anything good said about it because they want to destroy it together with the democratic system on which it is based.

Much can be done to advise and train people how to implement a policy of good human relations at work. Not every management will respond to the idea with enthusiasm, though nowadays every management will pay lip service to it, but it is always worth the effort.

In February 1989, the *Financial Times* published a review based on detailed study by a researcher at Warwick University. It was headed: 'Most big companies lack employee relations policy'. The study was based on interviews with the personnel managers of 175 establishments owned by large companies and with senior executives at corporate headquarters. The report says:

> *About 84% of head office managers claimed their company had an overall employee relations philosophy, but only half said the approach was written down, and only 23% said they gave a copy of the policy to employees. Most managers could not describe their employee relations strategy in detail.*
>
> *There is little or no evidence to suggest that the overall policy or approach which most of our respondents profess to have makes any real difference to their organisation's policies or practices. Most UK owned enterprises are pragmatic or opportunistic in their approach to employee relations.*

It is extraordinary that so many people have attributed much of Japan's industrial success at home and abroad to a particularly ruthless competitiveness and acquisitiveness, and to a highly disciplined, autocratic, if not repressive, system of industrial relations, when in many ways the opposite is the case.

'What we in industry learned in dealing with people', wrote Akio Morita, co-founder of Sony, in his book *Made in Japan*, 'is that people do not work just for money and that, if you are trying to motivate them, money is not the most effective tool. To motivate people you must bring them into the family, and treat them like respected members of it.'

I am sure that Mr Morita's success is not due to exploitation. I would deduce that what he says about how his employees are treated is true, because, as a result of my own and other industrialists' experience, Mr Morita could not have obtained the results he did for Sony if he had mistreated his employees. As he says,

There is no secret ingredient or hidden formula responsible for the success of the best Japanese companies. No theory or plan or government policy will make a business a success; that can only be done by people. The most important mission for a Japanese manager is to develop a healthy relationship with his employees, to create a family-like feeling with the corporation, a feeling that employees and managers share the same fate. The companies that are most successful in Japan are those that have managed to create a shared sense of fate among all employees, what Americans call labour and management, and the shareholders.

I have not found this simple management system applied anywhere else in the world, and yet we have demonstrated convincingly, I believe, that it works. For others to adopt the Japanese system may not be possible because they may be too tradition bound, or too timid. The emphasis on people must be genuine and sometimes very bold and daring, and it can even be quite risky. But in the long run – and I emphasize this – no matter how good or successful you are or how clever or crafty, your business and its future are in the hands of the people you hire. To put it a bit more dramatically, the fate of your business is actually in the hands of the youngest recruit on the staff. ...

Top management has to have the ability to manage people by leading them. We are constantly looking for capable persons with these qualities, and to rule people out because they lack certain school credentials or because of the job they happen to find themselves in is simply shortsighted. There is very little of the adversarial spirit in our companies, and making a living out of opposition to something is not possible.

The reason we can maintain good relations with our employees is that they know how we feel about them. [How crucial that is.] *In the Japanese case, the business does not start out with the entrepreneur organizing his company using the worker as a tool. He starts a company and he hires personnel to realise his idea, but once he hires employees he must regard them as colleagues or helpers, not as tools for making profits.*

Management, he says, must consider a good return for the investor, but also has to consider the employees as his colleagues, who must help him to keep the company alive, and he must reward their work.

> *The investor and the employee are in the same position, but sometimes the employee is more important, because he will be there a long time whereas an investor will often get in and out on a whim in order to make a profit. The worker's mission is to contribute to the company's welfare, and his own, every day. All of his working life he is really needed.*

Sony's success outside Japan is the result of treating its foreign employees as well as it treats its people back at home.

> *We have a policy that wherever we are in the world we deal with our employees as members of the Sony family, as valued colleagues, and that is why even before we opened our UK factory, we brought management people, including engineers, to Tokyo and let them work with us and trained them and treated them just like members of our own family, all of whom wear the same jackets and eat in our one-class cafeteria. . . . We didn't give a private office to any executive, even to the head of the factory. We urged the management staff to sit down with their office people and share the facilities.*

I have quoted Mr Morita extensively partly because I think it is important to understand why the Japanese have succeeded, and partly to rid ourselves of the notion that they have done so well because they have been operating to a great extent on the basis of fear, the fear of the employees that, if they do not work hard and toe the line, they will be fired and will not be able to eat. It may be recalled that after the oil crisis of 1974 and the inflation which followed there was great deal of industrial unrest, and that, though there were strikes in Japan, there were far fewer than in the United States and Britain. Many people attributed this to the alleged discipline imposed on the Japanese workers by their employers. I do not believe this was the case, but rather that the Japanese workers behaved so well because they had such trust in their employers.

I have enjoyed quoting from Mr Morita's book because I believe in so many of the same things he does, but I do not suggest we need to look at the Japanese example for everything or indeed for a great deal. Thank goodness there are many leading British firms which set excellent examples in industrial efficiency and good human relations. Moreover, I do not agree with every view that Mr Morita expresses. For example, he writes that 'If something goes wrong it is considered bad taste for management to inquire who made the mistake. . . . The important thing, in my view, is not to pin the blame for a mistake on somebody, but rather to find out what caused the mistake.' Personally, I believe it is important to discuss with the person or persons responsible for a mistake what went wrong and how to prevent it recurring.

There is another point on which I cannot go the whole way with Mr Morita. He says: 'I cannot understand why there is anything good in laying off people. If management takes the risk and responsibility of hiring personnel, then it is the management's ongoing responsibility to keep them employed. . . . When a recession comes, why should the employee have to suffer for the management decision to hire him?' I agree with and applaud Mr Morita's view that an enlightened company's priority should not be to maximize profits at the expense of the well-being of its employees; but to forego laying off employees whatever the state of the market looks to me in the long run likely to land the company (and, if others did the same, the country) in serious economic trouble from which the employees surely would be the greatest sufferers. If there is no job for an employee, it is not in his or his colleagues interest, or in the interest of the business, to maintain a so-called 'job' for him to work at. This, of course, may be an example of what is good for the Japanese not necessarily being good for the British or the Americans.

The same may be said for all employees, including executives, wearing the same jacket to work, albeit one devised by Issey Miyake, one of Japan's leading fashion designers. Not everything that yields results in one country is good for another, as we, the Americans and our fellow West Europeans all appreciate.

Nobody would dispute that there have been potent factors other than a good human relations policy and the practice of business responsibility to the community in the economic success of the Japanese and the Germans in the period since 1945. In the immediate post-war era the Americans made huge investments in Japan, in advice as well as in finance, and the markets of the Western powers – including those of the UK – were deliberately and systematically opened up to Japanese exports to encourage production from her renascent industry. Postwar Japan benefited hugely from this. But her people took full advantage of their opportunity, the human relations policies of leaders like Mr Morita doing much to raise the morale and efficiency of workers hit hard by the defeat and destruction they experienced during the war. They rose to the challenge and have never looked back.

It was much the same with Germany, another defeated and near-demoralised nation. Allied bombing had destroyed billions of pounds' worth of German industrial plant, rolling stock, rails and roads. At the expense of their victors, the Germans were given substantial assistance in rebuilding and restocking their industry with the most modern equipment available, while in Britain much of our industry was carried on for years with equipment almost antediluvian by comparison. The German 'miracle' was in large part due to the determined efforts of the industrious German people to re-establish their economic strength and social self-respect. But it could not have been done without the enlightened generosity and imagination of the Allies.

Among the benefits Britain in particular conferred upon the Germans was the inestimable advantage of a restored and reformed trade union structure. Hitler had smashed the German trade union movement. The Allies, mainly under the leadership of Ernest Bevin, rebuilt it on the basis of one industry, one union, there being only fourteen unions in all. To link industry to the community and to labour there were to be workers' representatives on the board.

In Britain in those years there were nearly 200 different trade unions, some of them feuding with each other as well as with employers, the whole vast field of industrial relations being troubled by the historic rivalry between industrial unions and craft unions, and between some of the craft unions themselves. These conditions, from which Germany was saved, plagued postwar life in Britain for many years and, in spite of much good trade union leadership, we continue to suffer from that legacy today.

I saw the contrast between my father's attitude to human relations and that of other people in my early days at work as a trainee in the Marks & Spencer store at Hammersmith. When I began my job humping crates from the trucks in to the basement stockroom, checking the contents and then heaving them up to the counters, I found myself working for a manager who had views about managing his staff which were very different from those I heard Father and Simon expressing at weekends. The manager there made it as clear to me as he could without declaring open war that he thought my father's ideas were rubbish. I managed to conceal my opinion from the manager, but one weekend I told Father about him and ended up muttering, 'He's a bastard.' Father retorted, 'Oh, you mean he's one of the old school.' He certainly was. It would be an exaggeration to say that manager ruled by fear, but he considered himself very much the old-fashioned boss. If anything was not perfect, he was critical and, if a job was well done, he never gave praise. There was no rapport between him and the members of his staff, and of course little between him and the customers. He rarely, if ever, used the words 'Thank you.'

Modern day Marks & Spencer might possibly have made something of him. I have learned since those days that, if he is taken in hand in time, a manager who is bad with his staff can be taught and reformed. When I was personnel director, I came across a manager who, though in many ways adept at his job, irritated his staff. His main trouble was that he considered his own ego at the expense of theirs and was censorious. When I asked his supervisors for their account of the previous week's sales, and they were telling me that they had sold about eight dozen of this or that item, he would interrupt and say, 'No, we did not – it was eight dozen and four.' This sort of interruption happened constantly as we went round the sales floors.

I looked into the situation at the store and found there was a high turnover of staff; some of them obviously could not stand him. I decided to remove him from the medium-size store he managed and make him deputy to one of our best managers who was running one of our bigger stores. He did not take too kindly to the move since it was a demotion, but he did as he was advised. He learnt a great deal and became the manager for many years of one of our largest and fastest developing stores, where he did an excellent job. Perhaps we would have had similar success with the Hammersmith manager if we had known as much then as we do now about how to help people to help themselves.

Good human relations at work do not mean being soft in one's treatment of people, but being fair and frank with them, giving praise where praise is due and constructive criticism when such is justified. This is important.

I have been friendly for many years with one of the most successful and largest entrepreneurs in western Europe. He is, in many ways, outstandingly able and a brilliant businessman. Often he used to say to me when we were together, 'I know all about your commitment to good human relations in industry, but I think you spoil the people who work for you. You're soft. Much of what you do for them simply is not necessary and it costs the shareholders a great deal of money.' To which I would retort, 'At Marks & Spencer we do not think of people working for us, but working with us. However, you're entitled to your point of view, and I'd be the last person to deny you've built up a powerful and profitable business which is famous worldwide. We don't spoil our people, and what we spend on what you call "spoiling" them doesn't cost the shareholders anything. It adds to the efficiency of the business, and so to its profits, and we do it because we believe it's right. Meanwhile, all good wishes to you for the continued success of your great enterprise.' I had this sort of conversation with him a number of times over a period of years.

A year or two after our last conversation his firm, which operated plants in various parts of the United Kingdom, was hit by strikes up and down the country. He became seriously concerned and asked if he could discuss them with me. 'Perhaps you're not so soft as I thought, and there is something in your policies. Are you prepared to send someone to look at our operation?' I agreed to send a senior executive, the number two in our personnel department, a first-class man. This executive visited eight factories and two regional headquarters, and produced a fine report, critical but constructive. Here are some extracts from it:

The personnel function is totally dominated by industrial relations. Whilst this is perfectly understandable in their culture, one was left wondering just how many of the fires that had to be put out would ever have ignited in the first place with a greater consideration of the human side of management. It was the technical side of personnel work, rather than the humanitarian, that was more in evidence, and the people employed in this function reflected this company requirement in their approach. An attitude of caring was not prevalent and I think would have been regarded as 'soft'. I met only one personnel manager who actually talked about their needs and problems.

There was a lot of responsibility for personnel matters vested in first-line management. Whilst this enriches their job considerably beyond that of a similar level in Marks & Spencer, it seems odd that minimal attention has been paid to training these people to deal with this aspect of their work.

There was a fairly widespread feeling amongst the personnel people I met that their work was not highly regarded by the chief executive.

He stressed there were certain activities in the organization from which Marks & Spencer could learn – for instance, about decentralization; Marks & Spencer is very centralized – but he concluded:

However, I remain convinced that the cause of many industrial problems is a lack of understanding of what people's needs are. Whether a company is capital or labour intensive, the human element will become more critical. To debate whether the problem is best handled by an effective personnel department or line management trained to understand human behaviour is irrelevant. It is more important to ensure that somehow the needs of all those employed are understood and satisfied if at all possible.

He asked me what he should do with his report. I told him to send it to the chief executive of the firm. The latter telephone me a week later.

'Marcus, have you read the report on us?'

'Yes,' I said, 'bloody good, isn't it?'

'Are you prepared to go on helping?' he asked.

'Yes, what do you want?'

'I would like you to second your man to us for a couple of years.'

'Not a chance', I replied. 'Here you are with a huge business with double our number of employees but you don't have a personnel director on your board. If you appoint one, our man would be prepared to work with him or her.'

A personnel director was duly appointed and the industrial strife was substantially reduced, more quickly than I had anticipated.

A few months later I was lunching with him in his office. The tone of our conversation was very different from previous lunches.

'You know, Marcus', he said, 'I have personnel problems in three factories. One is due to a shop steward who's determined to create trouble – we'll have trouble in that plant until we get rid of him. The trouble at the other two factories is entirely due to the stupidity of management who don't know how to treat their staff properly.'

What happened in the end to my friend's company as a result of our man's report? We know a little because five years later our man revisited the units on which he had based his report. This time he said, 'The business has made significant progress with its management style ...' Meetings of staff and management were frequently held, and the atmosphere was different. He found managers were using language and expressing concepts he had not heard when he had made his original visit. Meanwhile the profits of the company had soared. He was very pleased and so was I, since it was the best reward he could have had for the effort and work he put into the assignment. At Marks & Spencer we too learned a great deal from all this.

As I mentioned earlier, it is sometimes difficult to distinguish between what is done in the interest of good human relations and what is done by an enlightened management seeking greater profitability. In this respect my mind goes back to what I have learned about Volvo's activities in the early 1970s.

This renowned Swedish automobile firm achieved remarkable success in the period after the Second World War through the manufacture of cars and trucks, which sold widely in Europe and the United States. The demands of severe Swedish winters required automobiles equipped with a powerful engine, capable of starting reliably and running steadily in very low temperatures, a chassis which could carry the car through deep snow and frozen ruts, and a body and finish which would withstand protracted and penetrating snow and ice. These demands Volvo met, consequently prospered, and were glad. They were excellent employers; their workers were well paid, and were well looked after. Volvo had a chief executive with an outstanding reputation, trained in management as well as in accountancy, and with great knowledge of the industry – Per Gyllenhammar. All in the garden looked lovely.

In the early 1970s the picture changed, however, and Volvo found itself gravely threatened. This was not because basic costs had risen, the demand for Volvo cars had fallen or because production was being interrupted by strikes due to a decline in human relations within the industry. On these fronts business was going on as usual. No – the trouble was absenteeism. Well-paid, apparently contented Volvo's workers were not turning up for work. They would be here today, but not tomorrow; in for two or three days, then off for the rest of the week.

Per Gyllenhammar applied his mind to the problem. He found that the generous benefits paid by Sweden's beneficent Welfare State were such that a well-paid Volvo worker could take a couple of days off a week, go fishing, camping, gardening or lounge about at home, and still pay his way. Some Swedish employers, having discovered the same as he had, demanded that the State pay less unemployment benefit, so that the workers would be driven back to work. But Per Gyllenhammar had no desire to go down that road. He asked himself and his colleagues why some of their workers were so ready to down tools and reduce their standard of living. The answer, he concluded, was their dissatisfaction with their working conditions. They were fed up with standing every working day in the same place at the assembly line, turning a screw or pulling down a switch as the product passed slowly by on the belt, and immediately turning to put in another screw or pulling down the same lever as the next product came in front of them. They were bored. It was the repulsion of boredom, rather than the attraction of fishing, that caused these Volvo workers to become absentees.

'Machines must serve man, not men serve machines,' said Gyllenhammar. Volvo thereupon embarked on a massive reinvestment programme, the object of which was as far as possible to abolish the assembly line and substitute for it a different method for the production of motor vehicles. The new method began with the construction of a different kind of workshop, not long and narrow, as formerly, but shaped like a star. In each angle of the star a group of men worked on a major part of the whole automobile, for example the electrical system of a vehicle. They were jointly responsible for the safety and efficiency of that whole function. 'How can you expect people to identify with the product', Gyllenhammar asked himself, 'if they never get to see the product as a whole?' There was no assembly line or belt. When materials and tools had to be brought to the working group, they were brought on self-propelled wagons driven by one of their mates. When the job had been finished, the whole group would start on another.

Off each working bay would be a rest area, to which any of the group would go to relax when he felt like it and saw it suited the others. Each group chose its own foreman. His job was not so much to discipline as to organize. The discipline came from the spirit within the group and their feeling about the job. Each worker had several skills. They rotated jobs by agreement, so each worker could practise his skills and learn new ones. The aim was for each to have around ten skills. If a worker got fed up with his work, he could go to a kind of employment agency within the company and try to obtain different work, instead of having to leave the company to get a change. 'As they acquire more skills,' said Gyllenhammar, 'they will acquire more pride. As they acquire more pride, they will become more responsible workers. Responsible workers are contented workers. Contented workers are productive workers'. When he was asked if this method of production would not be the slowest system imaginable, Gyllenhammar replied: 'No, the slowest system you can get is when people find work so meaningless that they stop.' Would not this system be much more vulnerable than the assembly line? 'No, much less vulnerable than the assembly line. If one thing, one person stops, the assembly line, your entire production can stop; but, if one of our bays had to stop for some reason, all the others would carry on.'

So Volvo spent the equivalent of £2–3 million on the new plant. Many people thought Gyllenhammar was barmy. Some of his managers did not like the idea. Some of the union leaders did not like it either. But look at Volvo today: within its class as a manufacturer of vehicles it is the world leader.

*

In the late 1960s Sir John Harvey-Jones, then the executive in charge of ICI's (Imperial Chemical Industries) operation at Wilton, asked me if I would go there, have a look around and discuss the personnel problems he was experiencing since taking over this huge complex. 16,000 employees were spread over a 2,000-acre site distributed among seven different ICI plants. He felt that if he could improve relations with the employees the operation would be more efficient.

He and I toured the seven plants in the morning, and then discussed the problem of looking after so many workers spread over such a wide area. It seemed to me that an inadequate number of personnel managers were trying to cover too many people over too large an area. I suggested if one could divide the employees into groups so that one personnel manager looked after between 300 and 500 employees, certainly no more, then he would be able to establish better relations with those for whom he was responsible. It would be easier for John Harvey-Jones to have closer contact with his many employees either directly or through the personnel managers. He experimented along these lines and subsequently told me that the experiment had been successful and that his success at Wilton helped him in his career at ICI. He put this down partly to the good relations he established with all the employees there.

Some six years ago I was asked to speak at the National Federation of Building Trades Employers national conference. Naturally, I spoke about Marks & Spencer's policy and said that with the right philosophy and principles, even in those difficult days when unemployment was high, there were many successful and profitable operations in the United Kingdom. Afterwards, there was a discussion panel consisting of John Turner, president of BEC (Building Employers Confederation), who was chairing the session; Les Wood, general secretary of the Union of Construction, Allied Trades and Technicians; George Henderson, national secretary of the TGWU; Peter Rainbird, managing director of A. Rainbird & Son, Brentwood; Don Stradling, director of personnel at John Laing plc; and myself. During the panel session one of the two trade union leaders, I think it was Les Wood, said, 'If everybody behaved as Marks & Spencer does, I would be worried about my job.' Then looking at the audience of 180 plus senior managers in the building trade he added, 'But, I do not think I have anything to worry about.'

A number of leading companies have implemented for many years policies similar to those of Marks & Spencer with equal or greater success. An outstanding example not only in the United Kingdom but, I believe, worldwide is IBM. They pay great attention to the quality and value of their products, and fully understand the importance of implementing a policy of good human relations at work. When Sir Edward Nixon was chairman and chief executive of IBM(UK), he implemented the kind of policy I have described with huge success.

During my time in Marks & Spencer we did not do business with IBM, but I remember many years ago going to lunch in one of their plants, where all the employees lunched together and one could sense the spirit, co-operation and warmth that existed through all the ranks of people there. I believe similar principles are followed by IBM throughout the world in their great international business.

The following are some extracts from *IBM (UK) News* of July 1989:

The challenge of change was the theme of the IBM *Industrial Executives' Conference — Solutions for Industry — held in Bournemouth before an audience of 140 chief executives and senior directors.*

Opening the conference, Alan Willsher, regional director of IBM (UK) *noted the changes facing industry: government reform, open markets, 1992, demographic changes and technological advances. He then quoted Sir John Harvey-Jones's comment that not to change was a sure sign of imminent extinction. It was a point of which* IBM *was well aware. In 1962, Thomas J. Watson Jr. said* IBM *must be prepared to change everything about itself, except its basic beliefs – respect for the individual, the pursuit of excellence and service to the customer.*

Half way through 1989 chief executive, Tony Cleaver, was interviewed about the state of business by IBM (UK) News.

'How is business, both in terms of UK *sales and manufacturing? Some people say that* IBM *is a very different company from what it was, say, ten years ago, for instance in terms of respect for the individual. What would you say to people who are concerned about that?'*

'One could respond to that on two or three levels: I mean the first is that it clearly is not the same company that it was ten years ago, nor would it have survived if it hadn't changed. We're in an industry which changes faster, I believe, than any other industry in history. You only have to think back to 1979: we still had GDG *(Generation Data Group) and* DP *(Data Processing); in 1979 we did not have* PC *(Personal Computers) at all; at that time we had no volume discounts; and we didn't market through dealers or agents. So the industry has changed, the technology with which we are dealing has changed, the channels of distribution have changed. It would be amazing if the company hadn't changed as well.*

On the other hand, I really don't believe there is any less respect for the individual. I think if you look at the challenges the company as a whole has faced over the last two years, the most encouraging thing is that our fundamental beliefs – and particularly that respect for the individual – have actually stood the test. We've been able both to respond to the changing environment and to maintain those basic beliefs. We really have maintained full employment, despite the understanding that we needed a different distribution of our employees – that we needed fewer in some parts of the organization and more in other areas. We haven't taken the so-called "simple solution" – which, incidentally, I believe would have been the wrong

*solution – of redundancy, and hired different people. I believe that respect
for the individual really does remain one of our fundamental strengths.'*

Regrettably the history of the British motor industry over the
last thirty years has not been a happy one. The great British
success of the motor car industry in the United Kingdom this
century was Morris Motors Ltd found by William Morris, later
Viscount Nuffield. The history of the company from 1912 to 1952
was a story of development and success. The next largest British
car company was the Austin Motor Co.Ltd. In February 1952
Morris merged with Austin to form the British Motor Corporation Ltd, of which Nuffield became the first chairman. He
retired six months later in August 1952 and was succeeded by
Leonard Lord, the chief executive of Austin, later Lord Lambury.
In the *Dictionary of Business Biography* the section dealing with
Leonard Lord says this about him:

> *During most of his years in business Lord relentlessly rationalised
> production processes, the supply of materials and components and corporate
> administration. His priority was not the financial success of the enterprises
> he worked for, but extracting the maximum from the material and labour
> resources available to him. He was very ambitious, a ruthless pursuer of
> efficiency and production goals, a strong opponent of organized labour and
> left-wing politics. His brusqueness and directness were qualities that won
> respect rather than affection. He was determined from the start of his
> career to rise to the top: 'If the door isn't open, then you kick it open.' In
> the book* All Our Working Lives *Lord is described as 'the most
> dictatorial' of all the autocrats in the motor industry at that time.*

Unfortunately, the British Motor Corporation (BMC) was
plagued with industrial strife and profits were inadequate or poor.
The reputation of their products went steadily down. In 1961

Leonard Lord gave up the chairmanship to George Harriman, who had previously been the deputy managing director of Austin and had become a member of the board when BMC was founded in 1952. In 1966 BMC merged with Jaguar cars to form a new company, British Motor (Holdings). It was not a success. In 1968 the company merged with Leyland Motors, setting up a new corporation – British Leyland Motor Corporation. Sir George Harriman was chairman of the new corporation, while Sir Donald Stokes (now Lord Stokes), deputy chairman, managing director and chief executive officer, was responsible for 'running the company within the policies laid down by the board'. In the seven years from 1968 to 1973 inclusive the group's net profit was in total £200 million. It is estimated that the profits lost through strikes during this period was £92 million. In 1973 the company's production reached its peak with profits of £51 million, and a production of 1.6 million vehicles. However, pre-tax profits in 1974 fell to £2.3 million. The company was plagued with strikes and industrial unrest.

I knew Donald Stokes quite well. We had a number of discussions on the need to improve human relations in the British Leyland Motor Corporation if they were to be successful. A number of trade union leaders with extreme left-wing views regarded the troubled BLMC as a fruitful field for them to create further problems. When I discussed with Donald Stokes the need to improve relations between the management and workers, he said that, much as he wanted to improve relations, he did not have time, it would take too long to implement such a policy. He said, quite rightly, that he had to make BLMC adequately and quickly profitable, to which I replied, 'If you don't improve relations between management and employees, the company won't be adequately profitable.' I thought that he had inherited an impossible task because of the many years of poor human relations between management and employees prior to his leading the company. Those who had led the company had not understood the importance of working together with all those involved.

In the end Donald Stokes went to the Advisory, Conciliation and Arbitration Service, whose general responsibility is to promote the improvement of industrial relations and to encourage collective bargaining; but it was too late, for BLMC was virtually bankrupt. At the end of 1974 the Government gave a guarantee to British Leyland's bankers for short-term working capital of up to £50 million; five months later this was increased to £100 million. In 1977 Sir Michael Edwardes was appointed chairman of British Leyland, a position which he held for five years. In these five years the Government had to inject £1,740 million into the group to keep it alive. The efficient production of high quality cars was wrecked by industrial strife and poor labour relations. There is perhaps no more striking example in a developing industry over the past thirty years of how the failure to understand the importance of good human relations at work has cost the company and the nation dear in every sense.

Recently at the annual luncheon of the 'Think British' Awards I was having a drink with the former union leader Frank Chapple. He introduced me to a friend of his, an active trade union leader, who had spent a day that week at the newly established Nissan car manufacturing plant in Sunderland. I asked Frank's friend how he found the conditions there.

He replied, 'Outstandingly good. Relationships between top management and employees are first class. The managing director took me around, and we had lunch in the staff canteen. You could sense how good the atmosphere around the factory was, particularly in the canteen. They are all very pleased with their jobs.'

'Have you got many members there?' asked Frank Chapple.

'Very few,' was the reply. The reason was obvious: if employees are satisfied with the conditions of work, many do not want to join a union.

Nissan's production last year was 56,000 cars. By 1992 they will produce 200,000 cars annually, of which half will be exported; over 80% of the cars' parts will be made in the United Kingdom and they will employ 3,600 people, double the number they employ today.

The following is an extract from an article which appeared in the *Financial Times* on 1 August 1989 and charts the decline of the British motor sector:

From 1983 the UK *balance of payments has shown a deficit on manufactured goods for the first time since the Industrial Revolution, and the motor industry has played a key role in the slump.*

The motor industry trade balance has been deteriorating sharply since the end of the 1970s and has been firmly in deficit since 1982. In 1988 the deficit jumped by 53% to a record of £6.11 billion, accounting for 30% of the total UK *visible trade deficit in 1988 of £20.34 billion, and has worsened this year.*

Such was the depth of the slump in the fortunes of the UK *industry during the second half of the 1970s and the first half of the 1980s, that it appears unlikely that even the massive injection of capacity promised by Nissan, Toyota and Honda will succeed in entirely eradicating the sector's big trade deficit. The present large gap between* UK *new car demand and* UK *car production will be narrowed substantially, however.*

At the same time the UK *will begin to regain its earlier role as a significant car exporter. However, the badges on the cars will read Nissan, Toyota and Honda, rather than Austin Morris and Hillman, and, more important, the* UK *content of this new breed of British-built cars will be much lower than their predecessors.*

The drama of the fluctuations in the fortunes of motor manufacturing in the UK *can hardly be overstated.*

*

A good firm will make its philosophy of good human relations clear to its employees from the moment they join the company, indeed to potential employees before they do so. What Marks & Spencer does for its new employees may not be perfect and may fall short of what is done by other companies, but we are proud of what we do, mainly because those who join us say they are grateful for it. But one must always study how one can make further improvements.

In Marks & Spencer we start off with the conception that the first thing to do is to make the newcomer feel welcome. So, the moment a newcomer joins Marks & Spencer, he or she is handed what we call a 'welcome pack' with a personal letter of welcome from our director of personnel. The letter is about 200 words long and describes how Marks & Spencer stores are spread around the United Kingdom and the world, the company's basic attitude to staff, customers, suppliers and the community, and the prospects for promotion. It promises a 'comprehensive training programme which will quickly enable you to feel part of the company', and personal help and guidance through the personnel manager.

The 'welcome pack' consists of a number of brochures giving information partly about the company, but more about what benefits and opportunities the new recruit can expect. The information includes: the number of shops we have in the United Kingdom and in other countries; the number of suppliers we buy from; the number of countries we export to; where we rank in size among other United Kingdom companies; our annual profits over the last five years; the total number of our staff; the number of new stores planned; and the amount of money we have given to the community for what Marks & Spencer consider worthwhile causes. On the back page of the first of these illustrated brochures are the company principles, which we constantly try to apply, ending with, 'Fostering good human relations with customers, staff, suppliers and the community'.

A second small brochure, only four pages long, entitled 'Facts for New Staff', describes such things as how salaries are paid; the pension scheme; what to do in case of illness; our internal health services; staff meetings, held every four to six weeks and attended by elected representatives from every category of employment within the store, to discuss matters of interest with the management; profit-sharing and 'Save as You Earn' option schemes; sports and social activities; and cash awards to staff for making suggestions subsequently adopted.

A third booklet is called simply 'Jargon'. It lists in alphabetical order terms used everyday in Marks & Spencer, such as 'Arm' – a piece of equipment used on a rack to display merchandise; 'CSD', the customer service desk, in all stores to help customers with refunds, lost property, reservations, etc.; 'EPOS', the electronic point of sale tilling system; and 'RTM' meaning return to manufacturer – garments are RTM'd when they fail to reach the agreed quality standards.

We also issue newcomers with a booklet called 'The Right Move', which describes how to lift and shift objects so as to avoid unnecessary effort and risk of strain; and another called 'Personal Safety', which advises them what to do if attacked on the way to or from work or home. Other short booklets deal with other aspects of the newcomer's work. I believe that our new staff find this material useful; but I think that what appeals to them most is to find that the management wants to help them and make them feel welcome from the start.

I said earlier that good human relations owe more to example than precept, but I should add that at Marks & Spencer there is formal in-house training in human relations for supervisors and potential supervisors, these courses being reinforced by on-the-job training where the trainees put their new skills into practice under the 'sponsorship' of their management team. We attach much importance to the formal education of our management trainees but they also learn a great deal on the job. In addition, they have an attachment to the personnel manager to learn more about human relations in depth and are given specified reading on the subject. Their off-the-job training covers both the technical aspects of human relations (e.g. appraisals, interviewing techniques, handling disciplinary situations, communication methods) as well as their interpersonal skills, such as effective management, listening skills, teamwork, etc.

In addition to providing formal training in good human relations, we also train our staff in customer relations. We want our customers to receive high-quality service and we want to train our employees to enjoy giving it. After all, work that you enjoy doing is not nearly as arduous as work you do not. At the general staff level we use a great deal of training material, including videos. First, we deal with attitude, approach and knowledge of the product; then with how to handle complaints, the technique of selling, and how to give the customer good service at the till point and, very important, the customer service desk, a service which we are still trying to improve. Our supervisors get the same range of training, but in greater depth, and our management trainees get the same, but with added emphasis on the responsibility of management for the service in their units, which means mainly stores.

It is the manager who must set the tone and the approach to secure the right attitude to customers and everybody in the store. At the same time the personnel function must be integrated with the management function. To ensure this, our staff managers or manageresses in stores are required to take part in the practical running of the store, by which I mean its operational management. If they are not sufficiently involved in this, they become remote from the people whose welfare they are supposed to be looking after. If they are to look after their colleagues properly, they must share in their work. If they are not sharing in their work, they cannot share their problems; and if they do not share their problems, they cannot hope to solve them – and then they cease to be good managers.

My experience of the success of the integration of the personnel and management functions in these early years led me to campaign against the concept and therefore the use of the term 'industrial relations'.

The effort to obtain good 'human relations' at work is never ending, because example is better than precept, and it is how management actually treats the staff, and how the staff are seen to treat each other, not on good days but on all days, that keep the beneficial process going. Much of it is common sense. Some of it is enlightened self-interest. Some of it is the simple application of the golden rule 'Do as you would be done by.' There is also a place for training, which I shall come to later.

At this point, I might clear up the misunderstanding which some people still have about the attitude of Marks & Spencer to trade unions. Some people believe that Marks & Spencer is opposed to trade unions and tries to prevent employees from joining them. Neither is the case; anybody who works for Marks & Spencer is free to join a union, and some of our employees are members, though they amount to a very small percentage. I suppose that so few join because they feel the management provide them with as much and perhaps more than an active trade union would. Far from opposing trade unions, we provide them with facilities for holding meetings in the store. Of course we cannot guarantee an audience. In the fifty-five years I have been connected with Marks & Spencer we have never had a strike.

It is very important for employees to see that they are all being treated fairly. I believe people are more likely to be upset if they think they are not having a fair deal compared with the next person than if they feel they are not being paid enough, not getting enough time off, or are being overworked, especially if they know that this is being seen by others. This is very important in a work place like a store or an open-plan office where people can see with their own eyes or hear with their own ears what is happening to other employees. Nobody can expect to be paid the same as the next person if one wants to do overtime and the other does not. The young sales person cannot expect to be paid as large a salary as an experienced and responsible store manager, but there must be fair do's and these must be visible.

Related to this, all workers should be given the same consideration as human beings. The young sales person and the senior store manager are as human beings equal, and should be treated so. Many years ago a head cleaner working at one of our stores, who had put in thirty years service and had always been efficient and cheerful, began to show signs of unhappiness and depression. The staff manageress asked her if there was anything wrong; the answer was 'no' at first, but eventually the truth emerged. Her son, her only child, on whose education she had spent most of her resources and who had trained as an engineer, had emigrated to South America and was about to get married there. She could not afford to fly out for the wedding, and her son had not been working long enough to save sufficient money to pay for her fare. The staff manageress put up the case to the head office welfare committee with a recommendation. As a result, our cleaner was given two weeks off, her fare and her expenses were paid, and she flew out to the wedding. Not only was she delighted, but the people working with her were pleased too.

A few months later I was talking to the chief executive of a large British firm about the need for wide-ranging and flexible human relations. I mentioned the case of the cleaner and the wedding.

'You did this for a cleaner?' he said, 'You must be mad.'

I felt rather angry at the phrase 'for a cleaner', but remembering Father had preferred to say a manager was 'one of the old school' rather than call him 'a bastard', I contained my wrath and politely put this question to him: 'If you had an executive in your organization who, for some reason or another, was short of money and had a problem similar to our cleaner's, would you allow him the time off, and give or loan him the money?'

'Yes,' he said. 'An executive – that would be different.'

'Please tell me', I retorted, 'why that kind of thing should be done for an executive and not for a cleaner who had worked loyally for thirty years?'

The state of human relations within an organization shows to a great extent in the faces and bearing of the people who work in it. I do not say that in a Marks & Spencer store all the assistants will always be beaming like the Cheshire cat – they are too busy doing a responsible job – but I would be disturbed if I saw one of them continually looking unhappy and would (though the staff manager would have done it before me) want to know if anything was the matter. If people often look unhappy, the reason must be that they *are* unhappy, possibly unhappy with their job. Anybody who is unhappy with their job after all reasonable attempts have been made to help them in it should give it up in their own interests and for the good of the organization.

Good human relations should exist and be nourished not only between managers and employees, but also between employees and employees. One must not generalize too freely, but, more often than not, where managers set a good example to their staff, the employees will get on well together. Many of my friends and acquaintances who have nothing to gain by saying nice things to me about Marks & Spencer have mentioned how agreeably our assistants behave to each other.

Until 1973 we had two major British airlines, British Overseas Airways Corporation (BOAC), who flew the major long-distance overseas routes, and British European Airways (BEA), who flew the major European routes. Neither had a particularly good reputation for their standards of passenger (customer) service. In 1973 the two were merged to form British Airways (BA). In the ten years between 1963 and 1972 the two airlines made modest profits in four years, very small profits in three years and losses in the other three. In the sixteen years since the merger British Airways have made profits in fourteen years, particularly good ones in the last five years. Why? There is no doubt that this substantial improvement is due to the policies of Lord King, who became chairman in 1981, and Sir Colin Marshall, chief executive in 1983. Both understood the importance of quality of service and the vital part good human relations play in creating that quality.

I first became interested in BOAC when my wife and I flew with them to Barbados in the early 1960s. The flight, a long one in those days – about eighteen hours if my memory serves me right – was not pleasant; service was poor and the cabin crew unhelpful. I ran into some of the crew, including the captain, who had a two-day stopover in Barbados. In my talks with them I learnt that they were dissatisfied with the way they were treated. They said they had very little contact with those in charge back in the United Kingdom and felt that their suggestions and complaints were being ignored. They criticised the conditions of their accommodation in Barbados; criticisms, they said, which applied to a number of countries where they had stopovers. When I returned home, I contacted BOAC's head office and, as a result, was invited to meet some of the senior directors. I told them about the complaints I had heard, the poor contact between head office and flight crews, the poor quality of the service, and of the crew's dissatisfaction with the arrangements made for them in Barbados. One of the senior directors, who had some responsibility for personnel, said that he believed that what I told him was true. I replied, 'Well, why don't you go and see for yourself what conditions for your employees are like in Barbados, and listen to what they have to say?' To which he replied, 'Well, Barbados is so far away, how am I going to get there?' I simply could not believe my ears.

Nowadays, BA's reputation for good and helpful service is high. The chairman, Lord King, is always looking for ways to improve staff satisfaction with their work and thus passenger service. Here is an extract from the Directors Report for the year ending March 1988. During the year under review BA had bought British Caledonian.

> *During the year the company continued to encourage teamwork and communication between all of its employees in the running of the business. The 'Putting People First' campaign has continued through a new programme entitled 'To Be The Best', to which all staff are being invited. This programme concentrates on seeking from staff ways of improving the effectiveness of their functions and also determining how to tackle competitive pressures in a positive manner.*
>
> *A 'Welcome' event was held to which all BCal staff were invited, which communicated BA's philosophy on how the business should be managed and how staff can contribute to that process.*
>
> *Managers are also attending a week's residential course on 'Leading The Service Business'.*
>
> *A number of training initiatives have also been introduced including the 'Top Flight Academy', which is designed to develop staff with considerable potential to become managers or to extend and improve their management skills.*
>
> *Consultation continues to take place through management and trade union committees at varying levels within the company, where a wide range of business and employment issues are discussed.*

Much of the report deals with the way BA's staff are treated and the progress made. British Airways has been making much progress in recent years and is now among the best and most profitable in the world. In the last two or three years, whilst waiting for a plane, I have chatted with half a dozen members of ground staff who look after passengers; all have told me how much more their seniors have been interested in their work, and how much pleasanter it now is to work for BA.

Meanwhile, another major airline has been declining and this report given by a friend of mine of a recent overseas flight on what I shall call 'Blank' Airways is regrettably typical of the experience of a number of other passengers:

> I was going on the Blank Airways flight from A to B. At B I was to connect to a Blank Airways overseas flight to C, my destination. During the flight from A to B at the last minute it was decided to make an unscheduled stop en route to pick up some passengers. By the time we had picked up the passengers, the flight was clearly going to be late into B.
>
> I was concerned now about making my connection at B, and consulted the cabin steward. He told me that when we landed in B there would be agents to help us make the connection. However, when we disembarked at B, there was no agent in sight. The man with a walkie-talkie was very unhelpful in advising me where to go. In the arrivals lounge there was no information desk and no Blank Airways staff, and to my consternation the information screen indicated the flight to C had departed. Suddenly a stewardess from my Blank Airways flight walked past. Politely, I asked her where I could get information, only to be answered by 'I'm off duty now – I'm not working.' Would a little politeness and pointing me in the right direction have been so difficult?
>
> I finally found the Blank Airways checking-in desk, where they told me the next flight to C was leaving in ten hours. I was not even offered the use of the lounge or an apology. However, I did ask if I might be able to get

on another airline and was directed to the ticket office. Luckily, there was
a BA flight leaving that I could catch, and did. However, it was a big rush.

If only there had been a Blank Airways representative to direct me from
the flight to the ticket office as soon as I had landed, there would have
been little to complain about. As it was, the sheer rudeness and lack of
help from Blank Airways mean that if it is at all possible I will never fly
Blank Airways again.

From a passenger point of view, Swissair is one of the best airlines to fly, and is a successful and profitable airline. British Airways has joined this category, and I have no doubt this is largely due to the hugely improved relations between the air and cabin crews and the head office executives. The success of British Airways indicates what can be achieved by implementing a policy of good human relations at work, which Lord King and Sir Colin Marshall have done so well.

I can speak with some knowledge of these matters since several years ago I was invited to become a member of the advisory board of a famous international airline, once very successful. I looked at the list of the other members of the board, a number of whom had high international reputations and had been political leaders in their countries. Partly through vanity, but also because I liked and respected the chairman of the advisory board, and thought I could make a contribution, I joined. The standards of the airline were steadily declining, resulting in poorer cabin service, fewer customers and growing financial losses. My criticisms to the executive directors of poor cabin service were generally answered with 'We have little contact with our cabin crews.' Equally, my famous co-directors had little interest in the airline, and it steadily declined over the years. There is no value whatsoever in well-known names as window dressing.

Inadequate contact with employees and lack of adequate

response to complaints and criticism are signs of a failure to implement a policy of good human relations at work. Good human relations at work cannot be implemented by law if the spirit and desire for them is not present in those who lead organizations of every type.

In January 1969 Mrs Barbara Castle, then Secretary of State for Employment and Productivity, after discussion with the TUC and the CBI published a White Paper entitled 'In Place of Strife'. It did not meet with any success. After the Labour Government was defeated, Edward Heath became Prime Minister and Robert Carr (now Lord Carr) was appointed Secretary of State for Employment, and the Industrial Relations Bill was introduced. This was equally unsuccessful.

Good human relations so essential for successful and progressive business depends on the understanding of their importance and the genuine feeling for them by those who lead. The achievements of the successful companies described in this chapter were due largely to determination, a policy of producing and offering quality and value, and careful study of the market; but, above all, these companies were dedicated to a policy of good human relations with all in the business and had a minimum of industrial strife.

six

QUALITY, VALUE
AND DETERMINATION

Wherever the standard of living in a country is rising demand grows for better quality and value, not just cheapness. At Marks & Spencer we seek to improve the quality and value of the goods we sell. The progress we have made over the years would not have been possible without the close relations we have had with the great majority of our suppliers and the valuable contribution made by their and our technologists and scientists working together.

When I was a small boy Simon Marks gave me my first lessons about the importance of quality. We then lived in Manchester and Simon had already moved to London. Sometimes, when he came to Manchester, he would take me round the local store and talk to me as if I were reasonably grown up. On one occasion I went with him when I was eleven to our store in Oldham Street. I watched him looking around, picking up articles for sale, scrutinizing them and making notes.

That day I caught sight of a pair of knitting needles which had no knobs on the ends and held them up to him. 'Uncle Simon, how can you knit if the needles don't have proper ends?'

'Good,' he said, 'that's one lesson you've learned. Those are lousy goods; they should never have been allowed to leave the factory. They should never have been delivered here, they should never have been accepted and they should never have been put on display. Everything we sell must be of good quality. Quality, Marcus, is all important.'

I understood what he meant when he used to encourage me to become a businessman and often thought about what he said, but at first I was not sure what quality meant. I found the answer a few weeks later when Simon again came up to Manchester and stayed for a few days at the Midland Hotel, which then boasted one of the best restaurants in the country. He invited me to breakfast and ordered a kipper. It arrived under an impressive silver cover, but, when he tasted it, he said, 'It's no good,' and asked the waiter to take it back. He was served with another kipper; that was not good either and so back it went. A third kipper arrived; Simon took a mouthful and his face relaxed into a smile. 'This', he stated, 'is good to eat – it is "quality".'

Information is at the highest premium when it is collected at the point of interface between those who sell and those who buy. It is at this point that standards of quality can be scrutinized by the seller for the last time before sale. High quality is essential to good business, whether it is a service or a product which is being offered to the customer. The maintenance of high quality requires assiduous and continuous quality control. Many businesses have started well, continued well and then gone into decline because the managers have failed to live up to their original standards of quality or to develop systems for maintaining them. All the really successful businesses I know of have high standards of quality which they rigorously maintain, and all the outstanding business leaders I have known have had a high sense of quality.

For Simon Marks the word quality was almost a shibboleth. He was always in pursuit of it. Poor quality, for him, was an accursed thing. His angriest moments, and thank goodness there were only a few, occurred at the weekly Monday morning conference when on the previous Friday or Saturday he had called in at a store and had found on sale a product he considered to be of inferior quality. When we were all assembled, he would bang the offending article on his desk and condemn it is vitriolic and sometimes unprintable terms. The tone of his remarks would be of moral outrage, of a man who had been subjected to a personal offence, an assault on his reputation. This, indeed, was how he saw it. Quality, for him, was a transcendental virtue, an ultimate criterion, an ideal, except that in his view there was no reason, given proper management, why quality should not be commonplace, certainly in every Marks & Spencer store.

Being retailers, why did Marks & Spencer develop a scientific and technological team? In the early 1930s Simon Marks lived in Grosvenor Square, London, and frequently used to walk around the square. On his walks he grew friendly with his neighbour Henry Dreyfus, who became the head of the British Celanese Company. Marks & Spencer was developing its clothing business at that time and, on their walks, they discussed the possibility of British Celanese making a special fabric for Marks & Spencer suppliers. This was agreed and the first fabric was named V-30, and over the next two to three years V-31, V-32 and V-33 were produced, each supposed to be better quality than the previous one.

Simon Marks had a great feel for the quality of fabric and I remember one day in the fabric department seeing the four fabrics spread out in front of him. He fingered each one in turn and detected no difference. He said, 'Do we really know that V-33 is better than V-32, V-31 and V-30? "Vee" don't know and 'vee" are bloody well going to find out.' This resulted in Marks & Spencer appointing a leading scientist and technologist, the late Dr Eric Kann, who set up our fabric and clothing scientific and technological department, which has made a valuable contribution over the last fifty years to improving the quality of our goods. Eventually we had teams of scientists and technologists who covered the ranges we sold.

Our scientists and technologists are not back-room boys; they work with the buyers and suppliers, and have made an important contribution to Marks & Spencer's progress and success. Here again I must stress that we would not have made that progress were it not for the close co-operation we receive from the suppliers.

Initially, when Marks & Spencer's scientists and technologists wanted to visit suppliers, they were refused admission because some suppliers thought that Marks & Spencer intended to go into manufacturing and wanted to learn their secrets. However, in the end, they were convinced that this was not our intention and found our scientists and technologists of considerable value. Some of them wanted Marks & Spencer's scientists and technologists virtually to take over their development, but this we refused, saying that we would only work with teams which they themselves had or set up. Many had little knowledge of the latest developments in the technology applicable to what they were producing, but they soon learned.

In the late 1940s, after the Second World War, as Marks & Spencer developed its food range, to ensure the quality of our products we set up a similar team of food technologists and scientists under the leadership of another outstanding scientist and technologist, Nathan Goldenberg. The team has made considerable progress in improving the quality and taste of our foodstuffs. They are also responsible for ensuring that our suppliers maintain high standards of hygiene and cleanliness in their plants, and ensure that they are taking proper precautions against such diseases as listeria, salmonella and botulism.

In the early days we sold substantial quantities of fruit cake in various forms. Our bakers used some 4,000 tons of imported dried fruit for this annually. One of the major ingredients was sultanas. Despite the many precautions we took, we had complaints of foreign bodies, little stones and bits of wood, in the cakes. The sultanas were largely imported from Turkey, and in the end Nate Goldenberg with his colleagues made a number of visits there. They found that the method of harvesting the grapes and drying them so that they became sultanas had not changed in over 2,000 years. The bunches of grapes were cut and allowed to dry on the ground between the rows of vines. Whilst drying, some grapes would close around little stones on the ground. This was the major source of foreign bodies, together with fragments of wood which came from the cases in which the sultanas were packed and exported. Nate Goldenberg suggested to the growers that they set up platforms between the vines on which the grapes could be laid, and have them transported not in wooden cases but in cardboard cartons. As a result the number of foreign bodies in our sultanas was reduced by 95%. The Turkish growers concerned co-operated well and, as a result, received a premium price for their fruit – so everybody benefited.

Nate Goldenberg and his team did much to raise the quality and improve the taste of our foodstuffs. They also established high standards of hygiene, packaging and transportation with our suppliers.

At Head Office, Marks & Spencer have their own laboratories for testing the quality of fabrics, their wearability, washability, etc. In the food section, in addition to laboratory facilities, there are experimental kitchens where new or improved food items are developed, often in co-operation with suppliers. These facilities have proved invaluable as regards quality.

Under the direction of Hans Schneider, who was a leader in the field, we also set up a design and styling department, which works in close co-operation with our suppliers. Thus Marks & Spencer has a team of technologists and designers in textile, clothing and food who collaborate with suppliers to mutual benefit.

Of course one cannot rely on science and technology alone.

Marks & Spencer instituted wearer trials for clothing and eating trials for foodstuffs. Those who tested the items included members of the board and their families. Such testing is very important. One may produce items which scientifically and technologically are excellent, but for some reason do not wear or eat well and so do not please the customer. If the customer is not satisfied, the product has little value. But, even before we had scientists and technologists, we tried to maintain high standards and, if we could not buy the quality we wanted, we would not carry the items.

Two examples arise from the import of winter tomatoes, one occurring in the mid-1930s, before we had food scientists and technologists, and one in the 1960s.

In the mid-1930s I was put in charge of the produce department; this was before Marks & Spencer began dealing direct with growers, when we bought mainly from Covent Garden market. There came a period of two weeks in which we found there were no decent tomatoes available. In the second week I was asked to take to various stores – others as well as Marks & Spencer – an executive from a large United States food chain. We went to the Kingston area, where we visited four or five well-known food stores, in all of which tomatoes were being sold. When we came to the Marks & Spencer store, the American pointed out that we had no tomatoes, an important item, while the other shops did. I explained that we had not been able to buy any good tomatoes from the market, the quality was poor.

He said, 'If you don't have tomatoes for sale when your competitors do, your customers will stop buying from you even when you do have tomatoes.' I said I did not agree and that it was not our policy to sell any goods which were not of the quality we thought necessary. A week later good tomatoes became available and, after being without tomatoes for two weeks, in the third week we had record sales. It confirmed our beliefs about customer appreciation of good quality.

In the late 1960s we were concerned with the unsatisfactory quality of our winter tomatoes, which we imported largely from the Canary Islands. Although they were well coloured, they lacked flavour. I said to Jim Lane, then head of our produce department, 'Unless we can improve the quality of our winter tomatoes, we will have to eliminate them.' I asked him to visit our suppliers in the Canary Islands to find out why they were poor and how we could get better quality.

He spent several days with the growers and came back with the information that many tomatoes were picked green, unripe and hard, and hurled with great accuracy into baskets several yards away. They were then taken to the docks, where they were often left for several days in the sun on the quayside before being transported to the United Kingdom in ships with inadequate facilities. During the delay on the quay, the tomatoes coloured up; some became too ripe, whilst others remained hard with very poor flavour.

I asked Jim Lane what he suggested we should do. He replied, 'We should experiment by bringing them in by air.' Nobody else had airlifted tomatoes to this country before. I said it would add considerably to the costs. He replied, 'Yes, it'll add about 50% to our selling price, but we'll have good tomatoes.'

We brought in our first load by air. The selling price of the air-lifted tomatoes was 1/6d (7½p) per pound; the selling price of those brought by sea was 1/- (5p) per pound. Soon after the first plane load had arrived, I visited our Maidstone store. On the counter were those brought by sea, and, next to them, air-freighted tomatoes. The price difference was obvious. Both tomatoes were red in colour and the only visible difference was that the air-freighted tomatoes had a ticket saying 'Transported by air for freshness and flavour'.

I said to the sales assistant, 'I don't suppose you sell many of those at 1/6d against those at 1/-.'

'Mr Sieff,' she replied, 'once you taste the tomatoes brought by air you'll never buy a tomato brought by sea again.'

She was right, and it was not long before our customers realized it too. Despite improved shipping facilities, 90% of Marks & Spencer's winter tomatoes from the Canary Islands still come by air.

If one has principles concerning high quality goods or services there can be no compromise. Goldenberg, as I said earlier, was mentally incapable of any form of compromise in the fields he considered important. On one occasion we started business with a world-famous and long-established family biscuit firm. The head of the business did not approve of their making biscuits for Marks & Spencer under the St Michael brand name. Goldenberg, on the other hand, was not certain the standards of hygiene in the main biscuit factory were good enough for us. One night he stayed on there and, after the ovens had been closed down, he went back with one of the supplier's younger executives into the part of the plant where the ovens were situated. As the lights were switched on, hundreds of red ants, which carpeted the floor, scurried back beneath the ovens. These creatures thrived on the heat and enjoyed the scraps which fell on the floor during the process of manufacture. We immediately ceased business with this supplier. What had happened during Goldenberg's nocturnal visit became known; the chairman asked for a resumption of business with us, a request to which we agreed only when we were sure they had improved their standards to meet our exacting specifications.

Over the years we have continually tried to raise our own standards by training staff in personal cleanliness and hygiene; the educational programme is centred on the inculcation of an attitude of mind. In the foreword to the handbook on hygiene circulated in Marks & Spencer's kitchens and dining-rooms, it states: 'Hygiene is part of our philosophy ...It is based on each person recognizing his individual responsibility for carrying out the rules of clean food handling and the "clean as you go" principle. By the phrase "clean as you go" we insist that at all times the employee should give his mind to removing any kind of dirt.'

There are strict rules in our kitchens and dining-rooms governing the safe storage of food and the conditions under which it is cooked and served. Equally strict rules are agreed with food suppliers, both on farms and in processing plants. It has been rewarding to find that some employees want to reproduce similar standards of hygiene at home; complaints have been received from mothers about the demands made on them by their daughters. One mother wrote, 'She even expects me to wash my hands before making pastry.'

However, we have not always been successful in persuading all our suppliers to agree to establishing the standards we believe essential and so we have had to cease business with a number of them. At one time we did business with a famous firm in the Midlands which produced excellent cooked meats for us. They had been established for over 250 years and had a national, if not an international, reputation. The original family was still running the business and they made it clear, after I had visited them a couple of times, that they preferred me not to go on Wednesdays and Thursdays in the winter as those were the days on which they went hunting or shooting.

The area of the factory in which the St Michael products were cooked and processed was clean with good standards, but elsewhere conditions were poor: walls ran with moisture and the men's cloakrooms and lavatories were dirty and dilapidated, in fact Dickensian. I told them that they could not continue to have two standards on their premises; eventually the bad would drive out the good. I asked them to put things right. They were polite and said they saw my point. I thought that would be that, but, when I went back two months later, I found little had changed. This time I gave them an ultimatum: if they did not deal with the situation, we would cease to do business with them.

'You can't do that,' they retorted, 'we've become one of your biggest food suppliers.' They thought we could not afford to stop doing business with them, and therefore did not take me at my word.

I told them I would be back in four weeks. I was. There had been no improvements. I said, 'We cease to do business with you on Monday.'

'We don't believe you,' they said. They were not so polite now. 'You'll never cut out a million pounds' worth of business just like that.'

I told them we would. 'One day you'll run into serious trouble if you go on like this. We might as well stop trading with you now as wait for the inevitable. Anyhow, we don't want to put any of our customers at risk of eventually buying contaminated food.'

We ceased business with them the following Monday. Soon afterwards that long-established business collapsed; its operations were taken over by another large organization, but it was not successful and 1,500 people lost their jobs. The business had collapsed because the owners, rather than spending enough time and effort on the business, spent too much time hunting, shooting and on other pleasures, and failed to build up alternative management to operate the plant efficiently. It took us some time to replace the supplies we lost, but eventually we were able to do so, partly from British and partly from Danish sources, where our requirements on conditions of production were fully met.

Whenever we have taken decisions such as the one above which have caused us short-term problems we have benefited in the medium and longer term, while, whenever we have compromised on our principles, we and our customers have been the losers.

Perhaps one of the best examples of the demand for better quality and value in countries where the standard of living is improving occurred during a visit to Hong Kong in the 1970s. At that time we were developing our exports of St Michael goods. If a substantial proportion of the goods our overseas customers sold in their stores were St Michael goods imported from the United Kingdom, we allowed our customers to call their shops 'St Michael'.

Some years ago Dodwell, part of the Inchcape group in Hong Kong, was one of our major overseas customers. During a tour of the Harbour Terminal store, the largest St Michael shop in the group, I picked out five customers between the ages of twenty and thirty who were buying St Michael products. Locally made products were much cheaper, sometimes a third cheaper, looked similar, and were often displayed next to the St Michael goods. I asked each of the customers in turn why, for example, they bought a St Michael sweater at HK$125 when they could buy a similar locally produced line at HK$90. The answer from the five in turn was virtually the same: 'We buy these because the quality is better than the product produced locally.' (As the reader knows Marks & Spencer do not manufacture anything themselves, but are the largest exporter of British-made clothing; the company's export sales in 1988 exceeded £125 million.)

Another example of the demand for quality and value has been the development over the past twelve years of the firm Delta, which was established in Carmiel, in northern Galilee in Israel, thirteen years ago by a remarkable industrial leader, Dov Lautman. The plant initially manufactured men's briefs, and Mr Lautman wished to export to Marks & Spencer. Although it has been Marks & Spencer's policy to encourage economic development in Israel, it was on the basis that a product of similar value and quality could not be found in the United Kingdom. This applies to all Marks & Spencer's overseas suppliers. Even at the time of writing, despite the fact that the strong pound makes imports of clothing that much cheaper, 87% of all the textiles Marks & Spencer sold in 1988 were produced at home. However, Delta produced men's briefs of superb quality, made from long staple cotton, better than anything we could get in the United Kingdom. When we placed the trial order, I said to Dov Lautman, 'I know the price of your men's brief will be higher than anything we're selling because of the cost of the long staple cotton, but I hope it isn't so high it prices itself out of the market.'

The first time I saw the briefs on sale was at our Manchester store, where there was a bold display. I remarked to the floor supervisor, 'I don't suppose you sell many of those at that price.'

To my delight she replied, 'Chairman, it's a very fast selling line. You'll never wear anything else once you've worn them.'

They did indeed prove very successful. Since then our business with Delta not only in briefs but also in socks and towels, which they started to produce shortly afterwards, has increased considerably. Delta has found a world market for their products because of their high quality and good value. The result has been that they export to the United Kingdom, France and Germany 85% of their production, which in total at cost price in 1988 was £90 million. The cost value of Marks & Spencer's purchases from Delta in 1988 was £20 million, but we could have sold considerably more. However, Mr Lautman only accepts orders for what he can deliver; he does not make promises he cannot fulfil, and is steadily increasing production to meet demand.

Apart from the quality and value of its products, Delta is also an outstanding example of what good human relations at work can achieve. Of Dov Lautman's 3,000 employees about 1,100 are

Jewish, 1,000 Israeli Arabs and the rest Druse. He treats all his employees equally and in this expanding business there is much scope for promotion. He has made it a rule that promotion goes to whoever is the most suitable for it – Arab, Jew or Druse. He maintains first-class conditions for his workers, in addition to outstanding technical and design facilities. During the sixteen months in which the Arab uprisings in Gaza and the West Bank have taken place up to the time of writing, no Israeli Arab working at Delta has been absent from work on that account. That is a great tribute to Delta's employees and to the company's good human relations policy.

Earlier I wrote about the birth in the 1880s of Desmond's, the clothing firm in Northern Ireland; its main plant is on the border between Eire and Northern Ireland. Desmond's have developed into the largest textile operation in Northern Ireland and are a major, first-class Marks & Spencer supplier. Today they have over 2,500 employees, of whom approximately 70% are Protestant and 30% Catholic, all treated equally with promotion based on ability. Relations between employees are excellent; there has never been any friction between the Catholics and Protestants. In 1988, Marks & Spencer's confidence in the way Desmond's is run and in the company's products was reflected in purchases of £50 million at cost.

The bulk of Marks & Spencer's new stores and extensions are built by Bovis, contractors and builders, with whom we have now co-operated for over sixty years; we started working with them in the 1920s. They have performed outstandingly and they look after their staff well. Bovis is now part of the P & O complex and goes from strength to strength.

The management of Bovis have always been open to constructive suggestions. Some thirty-five years ago I took Simon

Marks to visit a supplier in Kent and on the way he decided to call at our store in Dartford, which was being extended by Bovis. After visiting the store, when we got back to the car, Simon decided he had better pay a visit to the washroom. It was a very cold, wet, windy day, so, instead of going back to the well-appointed facilities in the store, he went to the lavatory in the much nearer area where the extension was being built. There he found a rather ancient chemical closet and the construction workers were eating their midday sandwiches sheltered from wind and rain only by a tarpaulin hung over two girders from which the rain poured down. The men looked miserable.

When he got back to the car, Simon declared, 'Marcus, we wouldn't tolerate such working conditions in any of our stores. Although these people work for Bovis or their sub-contractors, they're also working for us. Some of those builders will be one and a half years on this site.'

On the way home he decided we should do something about this. That was on Friday. The following Monday the then heads of Bovis, Keith Joseph and the Vincent brothers, came to our Baker Street headquarters to see us. We discussed what we had seen at Dartford and what the implications were; we said that we would like to see improved facilities for their employees and those of the sub-contractors working on Marks & Spencer stores. Their reaction was first class. The following Thursday they met us again with a plan, the main feature of which was a decision that, when they built for us, the first building to go up would be acceptable temporary accommodation for the workers on the site: changing-room, lavatories and washrooms, kitchen and canteen for hot meals. These improvements added about 1% to Marks & Spencer's building costs. Bovis, who had always been fair employers, soon told us that they and their other customers had much benefited from what they had begun to do for their employees. For example, Bovis could thenceforth count on many of the casual labourers they laid off at the end of a job wanting to rejoin them as soon as possible to start the next. As a result, the workers were more contented and costs were lower for Marks & Spencer, despite the temporary buildings for their workers, because the speed and efficiency of the work improved, and the majority of building jobs were completed well ahead of schedule.

Another example of initiative and enterprise is the tale of Cavaghan & Gray, founded in 1912 by Tom Cavaghan and Jonathan Gray in Cumberland in North-West England; they were pig farmers and bacon curers. Despite severe financial problems in the 1930s, as a result of which Gray withdrew from the company, during the firm's first fifty years they built up a good business as a supplier of sides of bacon, sausages and cooked hams to national wholesalers and local retailers. In the early 1960s, during the development of self-service food retailers, their range was widened to include pork, steak-and-kidney and minced beef pies, and Cavaghan & Gray started to trade with major food retailers, including Marks & Spencer. In the words of Arthur Sanderson, the present chairman and chief executive, largely responsible for Cavaghan & Gray's development over the last fifteen years:

We now came into contact with a feature of Marks & Spencer which was then probably unique – their obsessive interest in every aspect of each individual product, especially factors affecting quality – quality not just of meat, gravy and pastry, but quality also of wrapping, print, outer container, production premises and distribution vehicles.

Refrigerated delivery vans were insisted on – a disproportionately heavy expense relative to the tiny level of sales in the early days. An early indication of the importance of the new development was the arrival one morning in 1970 of Marcus Sieff, who then headed up the Marks & Spencer food operation. This was the beginning of a business relationship which would lead eventually to the development of a wide range of high-quality chilled convenience foods and the creation of 1,700 new jobs at the Carlisle factory. There were big developments in store for Cavaghan & Gray. In 1970 Marks & Spencer established a national chilled food distribution system from strategically based regional centres – we called it the 'Cold Chain'. It was the first of its kind. Carlisle's location on the northern end of the M6 enabled it to be linked easily with the new depots. Suddenly highly perishable products could be produced in Carlisle and delivered rapidly, safely and in perfect condition throughout the Marks & Spencer national network, serving more than 250 stores en route, from Falmouth in Cornwall to Inverness in Scotland, 700 miles away.

In time Cavaghan & Gray's activities were divided into two, a meat division supplying bacon and other raw meat products, and a prepared foods division supplying a wide range of products like quiches, potato-topped pies, and fish and vegetable based recipe dishes.

For any business person interested in creative management Cavaghan & Gray is well worth studying. For example, there is no separately defined 'sales' or 'marketing' department; instead everyone is responsible for marketing themselves and the company to its customers. The directors, managers and technologists of the two operating divisions have the major share of contact with the customer, but they are also responsible for managing the staff and the resources required to satisfy the customers' needs. The aim is to establish a relationship, a partnership, to which customer and supplier are both fully committed, and in which the partners can exchange views and ideas in total frankness. Everything which relates to that is discussed, not only the quality of the products and the prices, but also technical and engineering problems, and the job interest and rewards for all the individuals concerned. The company is and always has been opposed to the development of a bureaucracy within its structure. Written internal communication is rigorously kept to a minimum. In a total staff of 1,900, only two and a half people are employed as secretaries.

A comparison of Cavaghan & Gray's figures for 1966 and 1988 makes interesting reading. In 1966 they were still old-fashioned bacon curers; in 1988 they were highly sophisticated producers of chilled convenience food dishes of most types. Their turnover in 1966 was less than £4 million; in 1988 it was £65 million. There were no profits in 1966, indeed there was a loss of £82,000; in 1988 there was a net profit of £3,200,000. In 1966 Cavaghan & Gray employed 300 people; in 1988 1,900. All Cavaghan & Gray's growth has been organic; there have been no acquisitions. Because the company's development is so closely connected with the progress of Marks & Spencer's long-established retailer–supplier policy, I may be forgiven for describing it at considerable length. Apart from our connection with it, I put it forward on its own merits as a remarkable and instructive story of how good management can develop a successful business.

An outstanding example of determination, courage and persistence is the history of the Nottingham Manufacturing Company, now a major part of the Coats Viyella organization, with which Nottingham Manufacturing Company merged in 1984. The business started in the Crimea in Russia, where Jonathan Djanogly traded as J. Djanogly & Sons in cotton goods prior to the Russian Revolution. After the Revolution, Jonathan Djanogly and his two sons, Simon and Jack, left Russia and spent a year in Turkey, before moving to Germany, where they went into manufacturing mainly cotton hose largely for the export trade. They located their plants near coal mines, because in those days the wives of miners often wanted work. They were Jewish and, after Hitler came to power and started his persecution of the Jews, they left Germany in 1937, having virtually to give up all they had developed since they had moved from the Crimea twenty years before. They decided to re-establish their business in Czechoslovakia. Simon Djanogly was sent to the USA to buy knitting machines to be sent to Czechoslovakia; his father and brother Jack were making the necessary financial and other arrangements to set up business there. The day before they were to sign an agreement with the bank, Jonathan and Jack heard a noise outside the hotel in Prague in which they were staying; they saw a column of Communists coming in from one end of the square, and from the other end a group of Nazis, each aggressively denouncing the other.

Jonathan turned to Jack and said, pointing at the Communists, 'We left Russian because of those people,' and pointing at the Nazis, 'we left Germany because of those. Send a message to Simon and tell him, if the machines have not already been shipped to Czechoslovakia, have them sent to England. If they've been shipped, try and divert them.'

Fortunately the cable reached Simon in time and the machines were sent to a site near some mines in Mansfield, Nottingham. Late in 1937 Simon and Jack started Mansfield Hosiery Mills Limited. They built a factory with 15,000 square feet of space and, with the American machines and twelve second-hand machines purchased locally, started production. In 1938 they employed approximately 100 people. I had the privilege of knowing Jonathan, Simon and Jack, alas all dead now, from the 1940s. They were remarkable people, and had great success. After Simon and Jack's death, Simon's son, Harry, took over the company and further developed it. In 1957, Mansfield Hosiery Mills purchased the Nottingham Manufacturing Company and subsequently refloated it together with Mansfield Hosiery Mills. In 1957, their first year as a public company, pre-tax profits were £450,000 on sales of £2 million. At the time of the merger with Coats Viyella, in 1984 they had sales of £250 million and pre-tax profits of £26 million. They were cash rich, and employed over 14,000 people in forty-five factories.

When I asked Harry about his family's success – 'modest success', as he and the family called it – he replied, 'My father, Simon, found it was achieved by hard work, very hard work, and bloody hard work.' The Djanoglys were not only exceptionally diligent but also people of courage, determination and foresight, who once they had the means, became great supporters of worthwhile community projects and very charitable.

I referred earlier to Robert McVitie, who over 100 years ago inherited his father's bakery shop realizing there was a great future for biscuits. Today United Biscuits is the second largest biscuit manufacturer in the world and is very profitable. It owes its great progress over the last thirty years or so to the dynamic leadership of Sir Hector Laing.

Since his appointment as managing director in 1964, Sir Hector's personal business philosophy – insistence on quality of product and of people – has been woven into the fabric of his company. Sir Hector, having come up the production side of the company, has always given priority to a constantly high level of investment in state-of-the-art technology, which enables his business, as the lowest cost producer, to offer consistent high quality and good value. Because he also believes in the importance of good human relations and in communicating person to person within the business rather than by the written word, he has built up and maintained an unusually warm relationship with a manufacturing workforce of tens of thousands of people. Necessary changes in working practices, which would have been considered well ahead of their time in the prevailing climate, were thus implemented and accepted by employees. United Biscuits, therefore, maintains its position as a high-quality, low-cost producer of biscuits and snacks in the UK.

*

All the firms about which I have written in this chapter strive to maintain mutually beneficial relationships – virtually partnerships – in their business with Marks & Spencer. Discussions between them and Marks & Spencer are frank and generally constructive; they seek to produce what we want and in turn we seek to find out what the final customer wants.

Personal contacts with and visits to one's suppliers are important, not only for good human relations but also as regards quality, reliability, etc. When I used to visit suppliers, I generally started by discussing with the chief executive the development of our business together, how it was progressing, what problems they were meeting, and how he thought we could improve matters. I would raise with him any problems we had encountered in recent weeks, for the head of the department concerned would be with me or would have given me a report. I then used to go on the factory floor, and the first place I would ask to see would be the lavatories and washrooms. Experience taught me that if they were clean and well maintained, generally the standards of the factory would be high. On one occasion, rounding a corner quickly, I heard the floor manager saying to a foreman, 'Look out, here comes Dan, Dan, the lavatory man!'

Good service to the customers is part of quality and value. Whatever one's business, nobody is more important to its success than the satisfied customer. Good human relations should exist between manufacturers/suppliers and their customers. This is important because it is fundamental to producing the goods which the customer wants and giving good service. Most of us experience enough unnecessary friction and indifference in our lives without having to take more of it. Whether one is a customer along the chain of production, a customer in a shop or a customer for a service, the customer is not always right, but he must not be allowed to feel when he makes a complaint that he is starting off in the wrong. On the contrary, he must be *treated* as though he is *right*. I have underlined these words to make the point that there should be no immediate admission of guilt on the part of the supplier, although frequently what is complained of will turn out to be the supplier's fault. It is important for a customer to feel that his complaint is being properly and seriously dealt with. And so it should be.

Not only is personal contact vital when dealing with suppliers, it is equally important as far as customers are concerned. When I am walking round a store I take the opportunity to talk to one or two people who are shopping, but one of the main methods of knowing what our customers are thinking is by reading their letters and listening to their telephone calls. Our customer liaison department receives about 2,500 letters, parcels and phone calls a week. Many of these letters and calls praise our staff and sometimes our goods; but the majority are critical. They complain, for instance, that our goods have turned out to be unsatisfactory; the ranges are inadequate; we are short of sizes or our colours are poor. Sometimes we are told that staff have been unhelpful or, occasionally, downright rude; sometimes that our store management has behaved in a bloody-minded way.

We are, of course, delighted to receive the letters of praise, to which we reply with a thank you, and we make sure that the store staff concerned know and are thanked for what the customers say about them. However, we take the complaints even more seriously, for the majority are justified. We follow them up and phone or write to and, if appropriate, recompense the customer concerned. If a customer is constructively critical, perhaps covering a wide range of goods, we invite him or her, sometimes a couple together, to head office as our guests for the day, show them round the departments concerned so they can see what we are doing and make their views known to the relevant executive and selectors. In the old days we used to reply to a letter with a letter, but we have found it is more efficient and economical, as well as much appreciated by the customer, to phone (if we have the number) as soon as we receive the letter, particularly if it is a complaint.

Sometimes we make mistakes. Letters get lost; occasionally our head office staff do not accept justified criticism; but in the main the customers appreciate the trouble we take to deal quickly and properly with the points they raise. Where someone has been poorly treated in a store, we arrange for the store manager to invite the customer in, make his apologies and give the customer tea and whatever recompense is justified. It is imperative to deal with complaints politely, efficiently and swiftly as this avoids losing valuable customers. Sadly not enough heads of business seem to appreciate this and their employees follow their example.

If one has a good product or service to sell, it is much more likely to be successful if the person making the sale is knowledgeable about the goods or services he has to offer. The discerning customer will want to know about the quality of the product or service concerned. Although poor quality goods or services will not lead to successful business, however well marketed, good service allied to a good product is more likely to lead to a successful sale, possibly a bigger one than originally anticipated. This means that, so far as possible, even the most junior sales person should know something about the quality and performance of the goods or services he has to sell. Regrettably, many people concerned with selling are not adequately trained and cannot satisfactorily answer the customer's queries about the product which he is contemplating buying. Providing one has a good product to sell, it is very important to train sales personnel in its qualities and value. It is equally important to accept criticism of products which for one reason or another fail to measure up to the standards claimed for them, admit responsibility and take steps to improve the product. There is much to learn in every field from criticism by customers – and the manufacturer, supplier or distributor ignores such criticism at his peril.

It is also imperative that sales staff are pleasant to and patient with their customers. Sales staff will generally be pleasant and helpful if they are treated well by those in charge of them. If they are not treated well by their bosses, they are less likely to be pleasant to their customers.

Like other businesses, Marks & Spencer seek to sell what the ultimate consumer wants. In many cases our suppliers seek to find out what the ultimate consumer wants by visiting the stores to see the customers' reactions to their goods. This is vital whatever the type of business. The emphasis must be on providing the customers with what they want. Too many producers still do not pay enough attention to their customers' requirements.

In 1960, when the late Christopher Soames was Minister of Agriculture, he asked me if Marks & Spencer would be prepared to establish a chair in agricultural marketing. Because of our interest in agriculture and in good marketing, I said we would be willing to help establish a chair, but would only supply 50% of the necessary funds; the remainder must be provided by farmers or farming organizations. I pointed out that, if Marks & Spencer supplied all the funds, most farmers would take little notice of the recommendations of the new department.

The chair was established on that basis, and it was decided to have a lunch in the House of Commons to celebrate the event. At the end of the meal I was asked to say a few words, so I talked about the need for the farmer to supply what the customer wants. After I had finished, a leading member of a well-known farming family who was getting on in years was asked to reply.

'I have listened with amazement to what Mr Sieff has said,' he began. 'Since when must we farmers provide what the customer wants? The customer must take what we produce.'

He was quickly silenced by some of his colleagues, but I regret to say his attitude was all too common in those days and still exists in far too many businesses today.

The high standards and success of the companies described in this chapter are largely due to thorough study by those in charge of their market, and to their determination to produce goods and services which represent high quality and good value. They are dedicated to implementing a policy of good human relations with all their employees and so have had a minimum of industrial strife. Those in charge have regularly visited their customers not just at headquarters but also at points of sale to check how their goods and services are selling and to find out what the ultimate customer has to say.

seven

MANAGEMENT ADMINISTRATION

Simon Marks was a great believer in what he called MBWA, management by walking about, to look, listen and learn. Other leaders of industry have had the same faith in this idea and method, but many have not. Not enough chairmen and chief executives, in my view, walk around their premises, visit the factory or shop floor to see and hear for themselves what is going on. Too many still sit isolated in their offices and rely on what people choose to tell them or draw inferences from sheets of statistics and columns of figures.

It is essential for a business leader to get good, accurate information quickly and frequently. One of the best ways of doing so is by walking about, although that may not always be possible or only up to a point. Any other source of essential information is bound to be second best. This emphasis on the importance of gathering quick, accurate information may seem exaggerated, but I assure the reader that insufficient and inaccurate information going up to the board continues to be a malady of British industry.

As well as developing a system for passing sound information *up* a chain of command, good management must ensure that sound information is also passed *down*. Errors of commission and omission at lower levels of an organization can often be attributed to a lack of information or faulty information from higher levels.

Inadequate information is a symptom of incompetent management. There may be several able individuals in management, but, if they are not using their abilities in the right direction or are not being properly led, then the company as a whole will be inefficient. Because competition is nowadays much keener than it used to be, such a company will fail sooner or later. Inadequate information is most likely to be found in a company or an organization where the people at the top are not as interested in the business as they are in their place in it. They are jockeying for power, position and privilege when they should be co-operating to make the business produce all it possibly can, and rewarding themselves only with their fair share. Co-operation does not preclude rivalry, competitiveness and some friction, but these should happen in the interests of the business, not in the interests of the individual. Co-operation certainly should not discount proper ambition, which is to do one's job to the best of one's ability and not to get on at the expense of somebody else.

In poor businesses there are often good people at lower levels. When taking over such a business, part of the solution to the problem may be to sack the top management and let the good ones lower down have their chance. This often works, but I repeat it may only be *part* of the solution. But one can say generally that, if a business has been doing badly over a long period, often the top people will have to go before the necessary changes can be made. One of the main arguments for this is that, if the majority of the former top men are not removed, they become an old guard, a court of appeal, a refuge for all those who want to resist necessary changes. Even if they do not want to, they will in practice often hold back new people coming up and frustrate them.

It has always been true, but the truth of it has not been as significant in the past as it is today, that an integral part of management is moral character. A person who does not display strong moral character will not be a good manager for long.

Either his company will find him wanting and, if he cannot readjust, he will have to go; or his company will be found wanting, will fail or be taken over, and he will soon be out of a job.

Leadership is vitally important at all levels within the company, from the main board to the shop floor. Leadership is the moral and intellectual ability to visualise and work for what is best for the company and its employees. Those who lead should recognize that what is best for the company and its employees is also best for themselves even though it is not entirely within their own compass but will ultimately be determined by the chairman and chief executive, who have overall responsibility and the final say.

To be effective leadership has to be seen, and it is best seen in action. Leadership must be communicated in words, but even more importantly in deeds, by example. More than anybody else in the company, leaders must be seen to be up front, up to date, up to their job and up early in the morning. The most vital thing the leader does is to create team spirit around him and near him, not in a schoolboy sense, but in the realistic terms of mature adults. Business is not a game, though it is highly competitive, between one country and another, between one business and another within a country, sometimes between one person and another within a group.

The responsibilities of a good manager are considerable. The more senior a manager becomes, the greater his responsibilities. Unfortunately, in some companies promotion is seen both by those who are promoted and by those who promote largely as the door to greater privileges. This attitude is not as prevalent now as it was thirty years ago, when it did great damage to this country's economic efficiency. More progress has been made in the last ten years than in any comparable period since the Second World War, but there is still room for improvement. One of the reasons why many managements were, until all too recently, able to jog along in inefficient firms and enjoy their comforts was a tacit agreement between them and their employees to live and let live; the workers would continue to be employed (even if some of them ought to have been made redundant) and receive wage increases, whilst the management continued to enjoy their privileges. Meanwhile productivity declined and costs rose. The price for this irresponsibility was paid by the shareholders in private industry and by the taxpayers in the public sector. The outcome for the nation was poor and costly production. This in turn increased foreign competition, inflation and, inevitably and most importantly, unemployment.

As I have said, information is essential. When an organization becomes too large or too scattered for one top manager to visit all the departments or different units in person, he must devise a method of collecting information which will provide him with what is needed. I know of chief executives of large, scattered companies who have versatile telephone systems on their desk which enable them to talk instantly to their factory managers. This does not give them so effective a contact as they would achieve if they were able to walk about in person, but it is a helpful substitute. All the same, the most senior managers must get around their plants and operations as often as possible.

One key means of staying informed and of maintaining control is the budget. Many people who work in businesses at lower levels do not appreciate the importance of budgets – the overall one for the enterprise as a whole and the subsidiary budgets for the various departments within it. A good manager studies the budget for the coming financial year to see if the sums of money asked for are consistent with the plans for production and the business's other forms of activity. If the business can afford the money, he approves the plans; if not, the projected budget(s) may have to be cut and the plans modified before the budget(s) can be accepted. After the budget is agreed, management studies the budget and reports on it at intervals, usually monthly, watching carefully for inconsistencies and deviations. Top management must tackle these quickly and ask for explanations; revisions in spending plans and therefore in activities may be required. There is a particular need here for swift and accurate information. Tardy or misleading information may lead to serious problems or a collapse before there is time to take proper remedial action.

Personal visits from a chief executive or head of group not only supply information but also stimulate the minds of those who are working in the shop or on the factory floor. It should be said again that good management is intimately connected with good human relations, which is a major factor contributing to the efficiency of a company or department; good human relations have a most beneficial effect on the morale of the employees and their performance. Most things a manager does are perceived by and affect his staff.

One of the most outstanding and successful managers of our time is Arnold Weinstock of GEC. When he was managing director of Radio and Allied, a company making various electronic products including radio and television sets, he used to spend as much time as he could in the factory and in the laboratory, looking at what was currently being produced, and at the designs for products planned to be on stream a couple of years ahead. He used to ask questions not only of designers, departmental managers and foremen but also of the men working on the bench, 'questions proceeding not from my knowledge but from my ignorance'. If he saw men punching five holes in a piece of metal, he would ask why it had to be five and not four, three or two. 'As a rule, it is cheaper to punch four holes in a piece of metal than it is to punch five and, if the operation has to be repeated hundreds of thousands of times, a great deal of money can be saved in the cost of production.' If he saw a metal fitting bent in two directions he would ask *why* it had to be bent twice, thus necessitating the expense of a second pressing operation. He might ask if the product would be any less efficient if the metal used were thinner and therefore less costly.

Weinstock has never been afraid to ask technical experts about what they are doing, because he believes it is part of the expertise of technical experts to be able to explain what they are doing. Unlike some people, he is not shy of asking questions which might show his ignorance because he believes that wisdom or stupidity are apparent in the kind of questions asked. He is not even put off from probing by observing that when he begins to ask questions some of the executives standing around start shuffling their feet or looking at their watches. He knows that in order to be a good manager he *has* to know, and has to be seen to *want* to know. For example, in the crucial field of quality control, if a manager does not maintain or improve the quality of the goods he is responsible for producing or retailing or of the services he is providing, sooner or later he will be seen to be falling short by his supervisors, by his staff and even more crucially by his customers. It is management by walking about to look, listen and learn which best assures the maintenance of good human relations, good quality control, and good products or services.

Walking through a store one day, I noticed that the satsumas were not selling. I tasted them; they were flavourless. Reports of poor quality soon reach the staff and the customers, who then do not buy them. A decline in the quality of goods for sale should be a danger signal to a manager. In the course of visits to other stores I tasted the satsumas; they too had neither flavour nor purchasers. I asked our technologists and members of the fruit department why the satsumas lacked flavour.

'It's been a very wet summer in Spain,' they said, 'and consequently the satsumas are poor in flavour.'

'In that case,' I replied, 'we should have stopped purchases temporarily, at least until the flavour was better, and avoid disappointing our customers.'

Some firms have an extra incentive to maintain the high quality of their products because, if they do not, the failure is immediately apparent to customers, who will equally clearly refuse to buy. Companies which sell food are one obvious example: McDonald's hamburgers have a high reputation for quality and depend on it to sell well. In a manufacturing industry making, let us say, electric kettles, the product can be inspected and tested several times before it reaches the packaging stage. A hamburger, on the other hand, reaches the customer as soon as it is cooked and can be just as instantly rejected. A few rejections publicly at the same time and place could play havoc with trade.

It is impossible to obtain and maintain high standards of quality if the gospel is not spread to the employees who are in the front line distributing the goods to the consumer. They more than anybody in an organization, including the chairman or chief executive, are the guardians of the company's standards and reputation. It is essential that they understand their key role, are dedicated to it, regard the product as their own and are accountable for it to the customer.

This takes us back to the spirit of a company and good human relations within it. The example set by top management is fundamental, but there must also be positive education of the employees, inculcating knowledge of the product and of the company's philosophy, right through the organization to the newest and most junior recruit. Indeed, the newest recruit is in a sense the most important person in the company at any given time since by definition he or she is the least educated and experienced, and therefore the most likely to fall below the company's standards.

There must be quality of sales and service as well as quality of product. Nowadays most successful firms have learned the lesson.

It is crucial for top management to use the products they produce whenever possible, and generally to identify themselves with what is being offered to the customer. By doing so, they get to know what is right and wrong with what they are selling. If a shirt is not good enough for the chairman and directors of Marks & Spencer, it is not good enough for their customers. The members of my family regularly, though not always, wear Marks & Spencer clothes, eat Marks & Spencer food, and drink Marks & Spencer wines. At the moment of writing these words I am sitting in my office in Marks & Spencer's headquarters wearing the first sample of a new model of shirt we are considering selling. Is it a good shirt? There is not quite enough room between the two wings of the collar for a tie; it is too narrow, by only one eighth of an inch, if that, but too narrow; so it is not a good shirt. This is a case not of management by walking about, but of management by wearing it about – MBWA in both cases. The problematic shirt collar is a matter for the supplier.

I said earlier that relations and co-operation with the supplying companies must be close. One reason is to ensure continuous exchange of information about the quality of the product. The retailer and the supplier should be in partnership, a relationship which best serves not only their own interests but that of their customers and of the people who work for them. It follows from this that MBWA not only applies to what a manager does in his own department or his own company but also to what he should try to do with his suppliers. It has always been important in Marks & Spencer that those concerned with goods and store operations should get out and about, making, developing and maintaining the closest possible contacts with suppliers, staff and customers.

The promotion of good human relations at work and efficient management are two aspects of the same thing. The best example of this I know is what we in Marks & Spencer christened 'Operation Simplification', a project in which I had the good fortune to play a major role.

The 'Operation Simplification' initiative was important in the history of the company not only because it saved us a lot of money but also because it enhanced our reputation. As a result of it we were consulted on administrative matters by both Labour and Conservative Governments, and on several occasions were asked to second some of our executives to major Government departments to improve their operational efficiency.

Like other businesses, Marks & Spencer aims to be simple and efficient in its operation. In the mid-1950s I happened to be in Simon Marks's office (he was then Chairman) when a leading figure in those early days of computers was trying to convince him that we should install computers in our business. When Simon asked this gentleman what a computer could do, he replied 'Virtually everything.' At this Simon turned to me and said, 'Marcus, we don't need everything. It's time we checked which of our systems are no longer necessary and what we really need.'

At that time I was the director in charge of personnel and store operations, so I set up and headed a small team to examine our systems, paperwork and general methods of operation. The team consisted of the chief accountant, a divisional director responsible for some twenty stores, an experienced store manager, a divisional accountant and a merchandise executive. Over the next six months we examined most aspects of operations at head office and in the stores. Although we decided a computer would not be useful at that time, we were able to make a number of major improvements. One of the most important changes we made was the elimination of the 'pink slip'. In those days a pink slip was produced in triplicate at the store on receipt of goods: one copy was retained in the goods receiving room, one was sent to the store office, and the third went to head office.

I reckoned that this pink slip had become superfluous and experimented with its elimination from four stores. I held monthly meetings with my team and just before the next meeting I visited three of the four stores from which the slip had been eliminated to ask the managers whether they had found any problems; they all said they had not and never wanted to see a pink slip again.

The chief accountant felt I was interfering in his area of responsibility and announced at the monthly meeting that the pink slip must be restored to the four stores. I asked, 'Why? Have you visited them?' He replied, 'No', but said he had been informed by his divisional accountants that stores could not operate efficiently without pink slips. I was pretty certain that he had told the divisional accountants to say this, so I pointed out that I had visited the stores and the managers were quite definite that they had no need for the pink slips. I then announced that the slips were to be eliminated in all stores during the next four weeks.

The chief accountant made no constructive contribution to the operation. When I asked him why, he replied, 'I'm standing on the sidelines waiting to pick up the pieces when you've finished destroying the business.'

After this unhappy exchange I told Simon Marks I could not deal with the chief accountant and suggested *he* should deal with him instead. Subsequently Simon also found him unconstructive and he was given a 'golden handshake'. After the operation was successfully completed and had become widely known through an exhibition we mounted and reports in the media, the chief accountant set himself up as the man who had successfully carried out Marks & Spencer's 'Operation Simplification'.

The examination of our operation led eventually to the elimination of 26 million pieces of paper produced annually (mainly forms of various types), to the introduction of a new method of bringing stock from the stockroom to the sales floor, and to the sale of over 1,000 filing cabinets plus several hundred time-clocks.

In those days Marks & Spencer's stockrooms were inside every store, as against the outside ones we have today, and they were guarded like fortresses. They were either situated in the basement or on one or more of the upper floors. No one from the sales floor was allowed to go into the stockroom to fetch stock required. Instead stock order forms had to be written out and sent to the stockroom. Then, in due course, the stockroom assistants would collect the stock and bring it down to the department concerned. I noticed there were often times when sales staff were not busy on the sales floor and could have got their own stock down, but when I suggested they should be allowed to do so, I was told that it would lead to major stealing. However, I replied, 'Ninety-nine per cent plus of our staff are honest, and those who are going to steal will steal no matter what.'

We pulled down the stockroom walls, thus considerably increasing the storage space, and allowed the sales-floor staff to select the goods from the stockroom. They knew better than anyone else what was needed to refill the gaps where goods had been sold and were able to go to the stockroom at quiet times. This freed 1,000 stockroom staff for other work.

It was and is against Marks & Spencer's policy to dismiss anyone other than for serious misdemeanours or incompetence; on the rare occasion when changes result in surplus staff for whom we cannot see further employment, they are given adequate notice and generous compensation. After 'Operation Simplification' I stopped recruitment for three years. Since 90% of our staff are women and they leave to raise families or because they reach the age of retirement, there is always some staff turnover. The net result of 'Operation Simplification' was that after three years we were operating a larger business with nearly 3,000 less staff, lower prices, higher profits and higher wages.

I have found that exercises like 'Operation Simplification' carried out by a small and relatively independent group are worth repeating about every five years.

The effort to obtain good human relations at work is never-ending, but, as I have said before, it is one of the vital keys to good management administration. Though the great majority of staff respond positively to what they see one trying to do for them, occasionally an individual does not. Some years ago I had to deal with a very senior executive who was failing to come up to scratch. It is part of good human relations to tell people frankly if their work leaves something to be desired and must be improved. This is particularly important when their shortcomings are likely to be visible to their colleagues and juniors, who are liable to be discouraged if they see that a manager is obviously not doing his job properly but nevertheless continues to be employed in a post of responsibility. I therefore gave the executive a warning; the issue was not yet declining profits, but a deterioration in quality control. The period of probation went by; his performance did not improve. I gave him another six months' warning, but there was still no improvement, so he had to go. It is another aspect of good human relations that, when somebody is required to leave, he should feel he has been treated as well as he could reasonably expect, and that those working around him should feel this too. So the 'golden handshake' he was given was a generous one, and he left us in what was, under the circumstances, a reasonable frame of mind.

Now and again it is necessary to criticise people, but rather than tick them off, provided you can leave them in no doubt as to what the issue is, I am sure it pays to avoid being censorious but try instead to appeal to the inate capacity for self-criticism.

Whatever you do, avoid making a mountain out of a molehill. My father had a genius for this; he was a natural diplomat. 'Give way on little things and you may get your way with big things,' he used to say.

eight

NOW YOU ARE
ON THE BOARD

Whether you are the chairman and/or chief executive or a member of the board you have added responsibilities. In some companies the roles of chairman and chief executive are combined. Large companies sometimes have a non-executive chairman, but in the United Kingdom only five in the top 100 do so; I believe there are more in the United States and in other companies overseas. The chief executive is responsible for the day-to-day running of the company and ensuring that agreed board policy is being implemented, which he does in co-operation with his executive directors, but when major long-term policies are under review then the whole board should meet under the chairman, whether he is executive or non-executive, and such meetings should include any non-executive directors.

The chief executive should meet regularly with his executive colleagues, both as a team and individually, and make sure that principles are being followed and policies implemented. When I was chairman and chief executive of Marks & Spencer, the board met weekly on a Monday to discuss developments and problems. The agenda included a review of successes and setbacks which had surfaced in the previous week. We would discuss, for example, whether action should be taken to increase the supply of fast-selling items, and whether to review the production programme of slow-selling items. We regularly discussed staffing problems. Were the numbers right, too many or too few? Were we meeting our budgets and sales targets? Sometimes we would find that the necessary action had already been initiated by the director or executive concerned.

At such meetings the chairman/chief executive should listen to his executive directors' views or problems; if in the end there is no general agreement, the chairman/chief executive should make the decision himself, taking into account the differing views of his colleagues. Executive directors and senior executives should not be afraid of *making* mistakes, whilst naturally aiming to make as few as possible; but one should be afraid of failing to *recognize* mistakes and taking the necessary corrective action.

The executive director must ensure that all employees in the area for which he is responsible are aware of the company's policy in that area. He should meet regularly with his people, sometimes in groups, sometimes individually, and discuss their work with them, give credit where credit is due, and clearly and frankly point out mistakes to those concerned. To be effective the director must get around, implementing management by walking about, to look, listen and learn. It is very important to build teams. Whatever the size of business, there is little need for secrecy; all employees should know about the progress or lack of it, of business failures as well as successes. Often too much is kept secret. The example set by members of the board and senior executives will generally be followed by those whom they lead and for whom they are responsible. Board members must make sure that they are not remote, that it is possible for all those for whom they have responsibility to have access to them. They should listen to the suggestions of those in their group, make trials of new ideas which seem sensible, and give credit where credit is due for suggestions which are successfully implemented.

It is equally crucial that those concerned, from the top downwards, have close relations with their suppliers and customers. The majority of successful businesses are those whose suppliers know about the policies which you are following and are kept informed of changes which are in the pipeline and may affect them. To do this effectively it is equally vital that one knows of changes which one's customers intend to make or seek, and to try as far as possible to anticipate these changing demands. I re-emphasize that close co-operation from the top downwards with one's suppliers and with one's customers is both important and rewarding.

Too often there was and still is too little co-operation between suppliers and customers, and too much antagonism and secrecy between supplier and buyer along the line of production. If this is so, it is ultimately the fault of the chairman or directors concerned. The supplier naturally seeks to get as high a price as possible for his product, and the customer to buy at as low a price as possible from the supplier. In the past this often led to financial difficulties for one party or the other and the end of business between the two parties. Members of the board concerned should see that such situations do not arise; both sides have to make a profit and, if efficient, should do so.

Today there is more understanding of the need for co-operation between the supplier and his customer, but still not enough. Both must know something of the operations of the other and work together to produce the goods at a price which will give them both a reasonable profit and at the same time allow the firm which buys from the supplier to sell at a reasonable profit and at prices which his customers can afford. Such a policy requires more openess between buyer and seller than existed in the past. There is rarely any need for secrecy between them. Such principles will only be properly implemented if it is the declared policy of the board, which the directors believe and follow, and if they ensure that those of their employees who are responsible for buying and selling understand and implement these principles.

Some years ago Marks & Spencer found its sales of footwear were falling dramatically. Those in charge could give no good reason for this decline. I wondered about the future of the department, whether we would have to eliminate it and give up selling shoes. I then decided to ask the heads of our major footwear suppliers to meet the heads of our footwear department for a discussion even though, in some degree, our various suppliers were competitors. I did not tell the suppliers that their competitors would be present. I opened the discussion by asking our guests why our footwear sales were falling. At first there was silence; no supplier wanted to say anything in front of the Marks & Spencer departmental heads and buyers. So I said, 'Gentlemen, until you tell us what is wrong with our footwear, nobody is going to get any lunch. And if you are worried about telling us our faults in front of the executives and buyers, thinking that, if you do so, you will lose our business, stop worrying. The way things are going there will soon be no business to lose.' The chief executive of our main supplier then piped up, 'Your shoes are too expensive, your designs aren't attractive to today's customers.' Another supplier added, 'We have not been able to convince your buyers and executives in charge what styles and colours they should try out.' Further criticism ensued. As a result the senior management of Marks & Spencer's footwear department was changed. We put on trial the new lines suggested by our shoe suppliers. Sales thereafter increased dramatically. Those originally in charge of the footwear department might have preferred it if we had blamed our troubles on the market rather than on them.

Self-criticism or at least self-examination is an important quality in any business whatever its nature. It is important to look at one's performance objectively, as there is always something to learn. If one is to be successful, one must admit to problems and face up to them.

Directors must ensure that they receive the necessary information regularly, but an additional and effective way of obtaining valuable information is, I repeat, by MBWA, to look, listen and learn. Of course information technology can and will provide a huge amount of information, sometimes too much to digest; but, properly controlled, such information is valuable. However, it does not replace the need and value of information obtained by MBWA. There are exceptions. A few efficient leaders sit in their offices and talk personally over the telephone to their executives, but rarely visit their factories or places of operation and are successful. But these are rare exceptions. Most executive chairman and board members who follow such a policy are not effective leaders. MBWA brings members of the board into contact with many people in the business and with suppliers and customers, from whom they can learn a great deal. MBWA is important also if one believes in the value of good human relations at work; it generally engenders a better spirit throughout the operation. Free, fast-flowing and accurate information is important for the directors of a successful company; one must not rely on information technology alone.

Sometimes MBWA can lead to unexpected developments and benefits. In 1971, when I was deputy chairman and one of the joint managing directors of Marks & Spencer, I made a visit to the North-East. In our Newcastle store I ran into Sandy (Alistair) Dewhirst, the grandson of Isaac Dewhirst, whom the reader may remember had in 1884 loaned my grandfather the £5.00 which financed the first Marks penny stall. Sandy Dewhirst was chairman and chief executive of Dewhirst, which had expanded enormously in the manufacture of menswear though it was still a private business.

Marks & Spencer had started to sell men's suits; it was a fast developing business. We found that the manufacture of men's suits had virtually ceased in the United Kingdom, so we had to import nearly all our suits from Italy, Scandinavia and Israel.

In the course of our chat in the Newcastle store, Sandy Dewhirst said, 'Marcus, we have a good deal of cash. Can you suggest how we might use it to develop our business together?'

'You do a good job in a number of menswear items but you've never been involved in suit production,' I replied. 'We believe there's a considerable potential for this in the United Kingdom. If you decide to go into suit production, we can help with design – we already have an outstanding Italian consultant and designer, Angelo Vittucci – but I think you'd have to import technological advice from Italy, Sweden or Israel.'

In the event Sandy and his colleagues decided to go ahead. They brought in a technologist from Sweden and, in 1973, opened their first plant in Sunderland, a first-class factory. At the time of writing they have three excellent factories with over 1,000 employees producing suits for Marks & Spencer with a retail selling value in 1988 of £45 million. Such was the outcome of one MBWA trip.

Another result of MBWA is that staff of all grades feel they are part of the business, instead of living in a 'we' and 'they' atmosphere, which is often partly the result of a lack of contact with higher management.

Some board meetings should be held specifically to discuss the physical and geographical development of the business, for instance what and where new factories or stores should be built, where to expand, what new services should be provided. Such developments generally require considerable capital investment. If the board decides on certain developments, particularly over-seas, it will, as I mentioned earlier, have to face the question of whether there are sufficiently trained personnel for the development without leaving existing operations thin on the ground. In expanding overseas it is essential the board ensures that a careful study has been made of the proposed development, geographical location, potential customers, population, competition, etc. I have already mentioned in chapter three our unhappy experiences in Canada, due to the fact that we did not study the Canadian scene adequately before we set up shop there on a considerable scale, and also the unfortunate consequences of the overextension of Mrs Fields' business. With hindsight I believe that, if a business is expanding overseas, it is generally better to have an experienced local man as chief executive there rather than select a chief executive from the home team. Of course ultimate responsibility rests with the central/main board.

There are some excellent executives who do not wish to become directors, but prefer to remain a senior executive. In such cases it is wrong for the chairman/chief executive to persuade them to become directors. Equally, there are occasions when an executive has been invited to join the board, wishes to do so and becomes a director, but subsequently does not pull his or her weight and fails to live up to expectations. It is then the responsibility of the chairman/chief executive to talk to that director frankly about his weaknesses and faults. Some directors respond and become valuable members of the board; others fail to do so even after further discussions, warnings and a reasonable period of time in which to change their ways. The chairman must be firm. Since most directors who are found wanting are not willing to go back to their former position, it is best to agree on resignation and give the individual concerned a generous parting gift.

Outwardly boards vary in their numbers, composition and in the frequency of their meetings. Behind the scenes they vary too in terms of influence over the affairs of the company. Some boards look very high powered, but in fact are not, as the result of window-dressing which has brought in well-known personalities who contribute little or virtually nothing to the business. Other boards seem to consist of relatively unknown, undistinguished men, but are in fact the mainspring of the company's activities.

The key figure is the executive chairman, who has a dual role: in his capacity as chairman he represents the company to the shareholders, the media and the general public, and, in his capacity as chief executive, he makes many decisions about policy and the general running of the business. Some chairmen are non-executive, and some are non-executive and part-time. Non-executive chairmen are less influential *within* their company than an executive chairman would be, though, if they play a prominent role in the company's public affairs, particularly, let us say, in its relations with the Government and media, they may be influential and valuable *in* and *for* the company.

Some boards are chosen with a view to bringing together a number of like-minded people and/or people with similar business backgrounds. Other companies prefer to have a board on which the experience of diverse business backgrounds will be reflected and on which many different, possibly conflicting, views will be expressed. Some companies, especially those whose boards consist of executive directors, are very much run by their boards. Others are run by a small executive committee of perhaps three or four members, who report to the board at full board meetings or refer to them if something untoward comes up. There is, in fact, great variety in the composition of boards and in the way they work. In my experience, generally the most effective boards are largely composed of an executive chairman and executive directors experienced in the work of their company plus a small number of experienced non-executive directors.

All boards, however, exist ultimately for the same purpose and have certain responsibilities which are legal and public. The first duty of the board of a public company is legal: responsibility to its shareholders, whose investment must be protected and properly rewarded, the activities of the company being conducted within the framework of the law. The board has responsibilities for the financial affairs of the company, for the treatment of employees –

pension schemes for example – and not least for the profitable development of the business as a whole.

Much has been said in the last twenty years about the shortcomings of British management. I agree with much of the criticism, though management has improved considerably in recent years. It is rash to generalize about what is wrong with our boards, and easier and safer to say what is right with them. What is right about our boards is that, on the whole, their members work harder and are ready to put in more effort than they are likely to be given credit for. What is wrong with boards is that frequently it takes time for new members to discover what they can best do to help, and sometimes they never get to know.

It might be thought that the best boards would be those consisting entirely of executive directors, that is made up of heads of departments of the company concerned, i.e. top managers, or containing a number of former managers, recruited either from the company or from outside. In fact, it is difficult to generalize. Managers, however able and experienced, do not always make good board members. This is because the role of a manager and the nature of his job are different from that of a board member. The prime function of a manager is to know what day-to-day operations are necessary in the area for which he is responsible and to arrange for people to perform them within the framework of what he understands are the general values, objectives and strategy of the company. He has a highly important job, responsible to his staff, his superiors and the demands made upon him in the running of a successful operation, whether it be a store, a factory, a division of the operations of a multi-national or the control of a service operation. He should know something of the general policy of the business and its activities, but his main job is to concentrate on that area of the business for which he is responsible. He must be prepared to speak frankly to his directors if he thinks their policies are not sensible.

The reader may feel like asking here whether there is much to be gained by having non-executive directors at all. Some businesses were and still are successful without them. In the developing days of Marks & Spencer under Simon Mark's and my father's leadership we had only two of what one would call non-executive directors: Leo Amery, a man of outstanding ability, who later became a famous cabinet minister in various Conservative Governments; and Con Benson, a great banker and a man of remarkable character who was shot down in the Second World War. It depends on the firm. Today Marks & Spencer have five non-executive directors, who make a useful contribution. It is wrong to generalize. Much may depend on the circumstances a company is passing through. To take a simple example, a firm which has been doing business only within the UK may decide to launch an export programme in, say, the United States and/or open up manufacturing plants in France and Germany. It might well benefit from inviting on to the main board individuals who have experience of dealing with related operations in these countries. Or, to take another simple example, a large company which has decided to diversify and begin to manufacture goods it has not produced before will benefit from having a new man on the board who is known to have had success in what to his colleagues has hitherto been an unfamiliar field.

How such matters and indeed many others of great importance are dealt with depends in the first place on the wisdom and experience of the chairman. Though legally the chairman is only *primus inter pares* and has no more legal responsibility to the public and the business than any other member of the board, his power for practical purposes is considerable if he is an executive chairman and important even if he is non-executive. I say this assuming, of course, that he is a man of calibre who knows his job, has experience of his company's activities, and understands the world in which it is operating.

It is often difficult and would not be right for the chairman to involve himself in the detail of the day-to-day running of the company, but he must know either through his meetings with his executives and departmental heads or through MBWA what is happening and about specific problems. He has to manage his board and he should be able to do so. He should have a major say in who is to be appointed to the board, who should be asked to resign and how many members of the board there should be. He is also largely responsible for the final agenda of board meetings.

The board minutes are important. In the case of a public company, they are legal documents and a time might come when for one reason or another the law may demand to scrutinize them. Though the minutes are not taken by the chairman, they are his in the sense that, when they are presented to him, he has to sign them as a faithful record of what was said at the board meeting. When the company secretary submits the draft minutes to the chairman well before the next meeting of the board, the chairman, if he thinks that something said at the previous meeting has been misrepresented, directs the secretary to rewrite a particular minute or to leave something out. The same draft minutes will be circulated to all other members of the board simultaneously and any of them may ask for alterations or deletions. All these requests or objections will be referred back to the chairman. When the board next meets, 'approval of the minutes' will be the first item on the agenda, and any director can challenge the minutes as they stand. Such a query frequently occurs and raises no problem, but, if there has been proper, sensible preparation for the meeting, there should be no need for it.

Dynamic chairmen in great or small businesses often want to keep the routine business down to a minimum so that the board can give its mind to the main direction and development, forward planning, and future strategy of the business. This is important.

While it is the role of managers to implement the company's policy, it is the role of the board to determine that policy.

A good chairman will not only encourage the board as a whole to keep its eye on the main things, he will also try to bring out what the individual members of the board have to offer, possibly by asking them questions at the meeting (or outside it) or asking for their comments. This informs the board as a whole and educates its members. Reciprocally, they should come to a board meeting with a clear idea of how they may be able to contribute or of what questions they want to ask. They should be able to do this as a result of reading the board papers sent out to board members in advance of the meeting and conferring informally with the chairman or with their colleagues.

It is very important that those at the top, from the chairman downwards, appreciate the importance of delegation right along the line to all who have responsibility. If those at the top do not delegate, the business will not be efficiently managed and those down the line to whom authority should be delegated will become frustrated and will be unable to make the contribution to the progress of the business of which they are capable. Proper delegation leads to the creation of team spirit, which will substantially improve an operation and bring out the best in those who are capable of taking on more responsibility. This will normally lead to a more efficient operation and increased profits.

It is often said that the ultimate test of a chief executive is whether, when he comes to retire, he leaves behind an able successor. It is certainly important to build up a clear line of succession by giving increased authority to those who should eventually lead the business. For many years, when I held senior positions in Marks & Spencer, I found one way of developing people with ability was to have them as my personal assistants for periods of one to two years and, if I found I had selected the right people, give them increasing responsibility. On the whole this policy proved valuable; with one exception, the very first I appointed, all my personal assistants rose to hold senior positions in Marks & Spencer. The one who 'got away' did not lack talent or ability: Bob Thornton ended up as chairman and chief executive of the Debenham group, a major British retail organization. Of the others Don Trangmar is and Frank Hirst was on the main board of Marks & Spencer, and several others are divisional directors who have played or are playing an important role in the progress of the company.

It is vital when one is chairman and chief executive of a business not only to provide for one's successor but also to do so in good time. As I mentioned in chapter three, I was fortunate to have met Derek Rayner shortly after he joined Marks & Spencer as a management trainee and at our first meeting to have appreciated his potential. Derek Rayner was outstandingly able and rose rapidly in the hierarchy. It was because of his abilities that I recommended he be loaned to the Government following Edward Heath's appeal for support from business to help improve Government efficiency; but more about this later. He succeeded me as chairman following my retirement in 1984 and has led with success the further development of Marks & Spencer in the past five years. He has not only further developed the company successfully in the UK but has also initiated considerable overseas development, which is leading Marks & Spencer geographically into new fields in the United States and elsewhere, one recent development being the opening of Marks & Spencer's own stores in Hong Kong.

I recommend my system of appointing personal assistants who show promise and to whom authority is delegated as they become increasingly experienced as an effective way of building up successors. I re-emphasize that it is the chairman/chief executive's responsibility to appreciate the importance of building up top management so that there is proper succession. If top management fails to do this, when the chairman/chief executive retires successful businesses have been known to go backwards.

nine

RESPONSIBILITY

Achief executive and his senior colleagues have wide responsibilities. I have described those responsibilities which relate to employees, customers and shareholders. I now come to the responsibilities which relate to the community, to the nation and to society.

Like other companies, it has long been Marks & Spencer's policy to give financial support to worthwhile community causes which benefit those in need of help, and also to second able people for periods of time varying from three months to two or three years to help in or lead various community projects. Normally the company has upwards of twenty people on such secondments. Some are very experienced people who are seconded for up to three years prior to their retirement; others are bright, young people who will not only make a contribution to the community project to which they are seconded, but will also learn a great deal which will be helpful to them and the company when they resume their careers.

In addition to ongoing support for community projects, about which local management is always consulted, the staff of stores have often adopted local projects, for which they have raised the money themselves. In 1982, two years prior to our centenary year in 1984, the board decided that in addition to our normal donations Marks & Spencer would allocate an extra £3 million in the centenary year to be distributed among local stores to enable them to implement community projects which they had themselves chosen, the only condition being that such projects should be approved by a head office committee. By the second half of 1982 the manager of each store knew the amount his store would receive for their community project.

In December 1982, walking round our store in Belfast with Maureen Millar, a supervisor, I asked her if they had chosen a project.

'Yes', she said, 'we're going to furnish a house, Ardkeen House, Belfast, which is being built by the Northern Ireland Council for Orthopaedic Development to provide care and accommodation for severely handicapped young people.'

Listening to her, it passed through my mind that this might be a rather ambitious undertaking, so I asked Miss Millar how much the store project had been allocated.

'£27,500,' she replied, 'but our staff are going to raise a great deal more than that. We've raised nearly £5,000 more already.'

I asked her how this had been done.

'Last night we sang Christmas carols in central Belfast,' she said. 'We raised £800.'

'Who is we?' I asked.

'We the store staff, Catholics and Protestants together.'

The Belfast store staff eventually added £48,000 to the £27,500 allocated by headquarters. With their total of £75,500 they purchased a mini-bus adapted for the use of the disabled, provided beds, carpets, furniture and a fully equipped kitchen for Ardkeen House, and helped to landscape the garden.

Lord Rayner has continued and expanded the company's commitment to its traditional community involvement policy. In the introduction to our brochure 'In The Community', which shows something of the extent and variety of our involvement and commitment to the communities in which we operate, he writes:

There rests on all companies, particularly large organizations like ours, a responsibility to assist through donations and help the charities and agencies which exist in the community.

The contribution that this can make to the community as a whole is substantial, and provides a lead for others.

In this field too it is essential that the operation is led from the top and that senior management show their enthusiasm for the cause. The Marks & Spencer effort is directed by the community involvement committee, which includes five main board directors. Three specialist committees deal with health care, the arts and community services, each of them headed by one of these directors. The company commits over £4 million annually to its community involvement programme, which is managed by eleven people. It receives 8,000 appeals for help every year, but we do not wait to be asked; we search for projects which come within our agreed policy. As well as giving money, we assist organizations with guidance on fund raising and management techniques. When we second personnel to help, we try to choose the person with the right qualities for a particular project. We provide him or her with back-up services and maintain close links with them. We have always hoped that the secondee, as well as the organization, would benefit from the secondment and our hopes have been justified.

Our arts programme tries to reach as wide an audience as possible throughout the UK. We help to take the arts into the community, particularly making them available to the handicapped and the elderly. MacIntyre School runs several homes and schools for the mentally handicapped; we have provided them with various equipment including, for example, a piano for one of their homes. We have financed the replacement of worn out musical instruments at the Sam Sharpe Music Workshop in Wolverhampton. We are a major sponsor of the National Festival of Music for Youth. We give generous financial support to our cultural heritage through museums, restoration programmes and conservation.

The problems of the inner cities and other areas of deprivation have loomed large in the past decade. We have been involved in the Youth Training Scheme from its inception in 1983, running a pilot course for the Manpower Services Commission in twelve of our northern stores in 1982. We support the Prince's Youth Business Trust, which does invaluable work providing finance, professional advice and training to assist eighteen- to twenty-five-year-olds in setting up their own small businesses. In further education, we primarily sponsor schemes which have relevance to our own business.

We are particularly active in the field of health. We support the development of medical knowledge and techniques, consulting our own doctors as well as outside specialists to find out whether and how much we can help. We put a high priority on helping the elderly. For two years we gave special assistance to the Help the Aged Lifeline Alarm Appeal in the provision of alarm systems for elderly people who live alone. We give support to hospices and research programmes involving the elderly. We have contributed towards the running costs of the department of care for the elderly at Frenchay established by the University of Bristol. We are contributing towards the running costs of a three-year study for the benefit of victims of alcohol and drug abuse set up by Professor Anthony Clare of St Bartholomew's Hospital, and to the conversion of Lorne House in one of the most deprived areas in London into a treatment centre for them. We make contributions to cancer research and also to the British Association of Cancer United Patients (BACUP), which offers counselling and support to cancer sufferers and their families all over the UK.

In addition, as I briefly mentioned earlier, the company is

actively concerned with maintaining and improving the health of
its employees. The following is a report by Dr Taylor, chief
medical officer of Marks & Spencer on the company's activities
for all employees:

*As part of the company's good human relations policy and real concern
for the well-being of all staff, a wide range of health services has been offered
to all employees for many years.*

*All health care programmes have been based on a team approach –
through a network of doctors, nurses, dentists, chiropodists, physiotherapists
and other health professionals. Their underlying philosophy is that whenever
possible, prevention is better than cure and early treatment better than late.
In the simplest terms, this means readily available advice on health related
problems; in wider terms, attention to the health and safety of the work
environment, with all the changes implicit in new technology, and the
provision of health promotion through education, screening programmes and
continuing follow-up through action and intervention, always based on the
principle of freedom of choice, of guided self-help to better health.*

*Thus, staff have been offered health education in order to increase the
awareness of factors which may affect health and well-being. The screening
programmes are targeted at diseases which cause a high level of sickness
and premature death.*

*Therefore, in 1968, Marks & Spencer pioneered the provision of cervical
smears at work in order to detect cancer of the neck of the womb at an
early and more successfully treatable stage. In 1973, a programme was
initiated to detect cancer of the breast at an early stage. Over the years,
around 80% or more of those eligible have joined these programmes, which
continue to be offered at work free of charge, and modified appropriately
in the light of current medical knowledge.*

*More recently, an ambitious programme has been launched for the
detection of risk factors for another major scourge of our times, coronary
heart disease. Offered to the over 30s, over 90% have taken part and we*

hope that the beneficial impact will be felt as the years go by.

All these services are regularly reviewed and revised appropriately so that they remain right for their times and for the needs of the customers of Health Services – all who work for Marks & Spencer.

A number of companies have somewhat similar and equally successful medical programmes. I have gone into detail on the medical facilities Marks & Spencer have established over the years to maintain and improve the health of all employees in the hope that it will encourage other firms, no matter how small, to do likewise. If every business had a health care programme think what a difference it would make in human and economic terms. The United Kingdom workforce has one of the highest records of absenteeism for a modern industrial country.

We have always felt a great sense of responsibility for the standard of the food we sell and the hygiene which goes with it. Cleanliness, purity and safety have figured prominently in general policy. There was a great need for progress after the Second World War when many Marks & Spencer stores had to accept lower standards than they would have wished because of the restrictions and shortages imposed by the exigencies of the war years. An excellent brief account of what remedial work was necessary, which was done as soon as possible, is provided by Nate Goldenberg, Marks & Spencer's chief food consultant for over twenty years, in his book *Thought For Food*. Nate emphasized the necessity for top management to set an enthusiastic example, a necessity which I have emphasized in other fields in earlier parts of this book.

For the attainment of good standards of hygiene in a food factory, as indeed in all fields of endeavour, the involvement of top management is essential. Without this, all efforts by the hygiene officer and even by middle management, are unlikely to succeed. Top management should make it clear that the up-keep of good hygiene standards should be part and parcel of the mental make-up of all involved – management, middle management, technologists, floor managers, supervisors, foremen and operatives. . . .

Top management should 'make' the time to visit the factory floor during production and look closely at standards of hygiene (and also of quality and quality control). It is very important for top management not only to be interested but to be seen to be interested both at meetings and in visits to the factory floor.

In another part of his book, Nate wrote of the problem of getting certain attitudes and standards accepted by our various departments:

Because the food technologists were 'seconded' to the buying departments and shared the same office, the buyers began to understand and then appreciate the value of technology in their work. This took time. In my early days at Marks & Spencer, this was certainly not so – it developed gradually; the buyers found that the technologists had a contribution to make on quality standards; on customer complaints of 'off-flavours' and 'off-odours'; on quality control; on the right use of raw materials and packaging; and on the development of new lines and new ideas.

At first, the idea of finite 'shelf-life' was not easily accepted by the merchandisers; and it was only gradually they realised its importance in maintaining quality standards. The same can be said of the development of the 'cold chain' techniques used in the handling of 'high-risk' foods, and of fresh salads and vegetables. Both ideas were at the time novel and indeed revolutionary; Marks & Spencer pioneered their development on a commercial scale and the rest of the food industry followed. Today it is routine and widely used.

The idea that foods of high quality cannot be produced in dirty factories under unhygienic conditions was also accepted only gradually by the mer-

chandising departments, but in the end it was understood and discussed on all visits to suppliers. Indeed, it became 'everybody's' business. The 'gospel' of hygienic food handling was preached by Marks & Spencer food personnel, not only at suppliers but also in the Marks & Spencer stores, in their staff canteens and welfare facilities (cloakroom, toilets, etc.), in their stockrooms and indeed even in outside hotels and restaurants!

Of course, this would not have been achieved had it not been made clear to everybody that the sensible use of technology and technological 'know-how' was board policy; it was often emphasised personally by Simon Marks, Israel Sieff and above all by Marcus Sieff in their many meetings with people in the food division.

Last year, in response to scares about dangerous 'presences' in foods – bits of glass in baby foods, metal in baked beans, listeria in soft cheeses and paté – the Government published its White Paper on food safety. Marks & Spencer were gratified when, in the *Financial Times*, Rachel Johnson wrote a long and thorough piece about the company's techniques for keeping food safe, describing it as an example to be followed and taking as her text the citation by the Commons' social services committee of Marks & Spencer as 'a model of good practices other manufacturers and retailers should aspire to'.

More recently a sense of responsibility for food has taken the company increasingly into the field of organic foods, like flour, fruit, vegetables, free-range chickens, eggs, and so on. Great strides have been made in organic produce generally. The range consists of major produce lines specially selected for Marks & Spencer, which have achieved the high standards of quality associated with the brand name. According to season, most main popular vegetables, fruits and salads are available. All the packaging is environmentally friendly and carries the Soil Association's logo. The trays are made from 100% biodegradable, unbleached wood pulp, and the film is plasticizer free.

Chicken, eggs, pork and veal receive special attention. Following the national success of free-range whole chicken and fillets, a trial of portions has been launched in several Marks & Spencer stores. The range includes drumsticks, thighs and legs as well as bone-in and boneless breasts. The system was created to simulate, as closely as possible, a return to the best traditional farming practices. The methods of producing our free-range chickens are much the same as they were fifty years ago. Farmers employ traditional husbandry to raise the chickens. Farms are regularly visited to provide assistance and advice and to ensure that our high standards, and those of our supplier, are being met. Free-range chickens are reared in fields which are natural, untreated and chemical free, and are fed on a diet of wheat, soya and vegetable oil.

Marks & Spencer were one of the first retailers to offer free-range eggs nationwide. All free-range eggs supplied by Marks & Spencer are from hens reared at no more than 450 birds per acre with unlimited access to the outdoors during daylight hours.

So much for environmental foods. Other products also reflect the firm's sense of responsibility to the community. Aerosols, for example: all St Michael aerosols are CFC (chloro fluoro carbon) free, all of them carry an 'ozone friendly' sticker, and pump and trigger sprays are also available. All foam fillings used in St Michael furniture are CFC free. The amount of polyethylene in carrier bags has been reduced to save on energy and resources, while still retaining strength. All new food carrier bags are being printed with 'Please re-use in the interest of the environment'. All new Marks & Spencer refrigeration will operate with the most ozone friendly refrigerant, R22. In addition, equipment suppliers have confirmed their commitment and ensure that current installation and maintenance procedures prevent accidental release of CFC gases into the atmosphere. All St Michael washing powders are highly concentrated and contain approximately 30% less phosphates than conventional E10 and E20 powders. We are currently investigating phosphate-free washing powders and liquid washes. The detergents used in all St Michael homecare laundry products are readily biodegradable. Our products use detergents which exceed the requirement of 80% biodegradation in legal terms. St Michael rim block lavatory deodorizers do not contain PDCB (Paradichlorobenzene). The dioxin content of our products has been independently analysed, and we are assured on the basis of barely detectable levels that our products are safe and will cause no harm to the customer.

There is also much concern today about the use of timber from tropical rain forests. Some items of St Michael furniture are manufactured from tropical rain forest hardwoods, mahogany for example, but to minimize the use of such woods veneers are used. We also have mahogany finish products, bathroom cabinets for example, which are made from pine, but are stained to look like mahogany. We are not developing any new ranges containing rain forest timber. We are currently seeking alternatives and sourcing from other areas to replace mahogany with other woods which are ecologically sound or come from sustainable sources. Teak used in our garden furniture is taken from plantations cultivated, cropped and replanted to supply this wood. We have discontinued iroko wood garden furniture.

To conserve and improve the environment generally the concerned business person must not only do what he or she can, but help others to do so as well, not only spread the gospel but spread the wherewithal. Marks & Spencer sponsor the Groundwork Foundation, which improves landscapes in urban fringe areas, and we provided it with £37,500 to initiate a project to encourage young people in deprived areas to improve their environment. £25,000 was granted to the British Trust of Conservation Volunteers, which trains volunteers to tackle a wide range of projects.

We work closely with the local councils and landscape artists when developing new sites, and pay particular attention to stores being aesthetically pleasing and in keeping with the setting and ambience of the particular town. Most of our development programme consists of improving existing sites. We have a few edge-of-town sites, where we have employed an ecologist to advise on environmental issues. It is the policy of Marks & Spencer not to consider new sites or developments which would infringe upon the Green Belt.

We are one of the most pro-active retailers in the sponsorship of litter bins. We not only give financial assistance but also involve the local authorities and other retailers in helping to keep our towns clean, pleasanter and safer. Where stores are built near sites of historical interest, we not only offer archaeologists the chance to dig before our building work commences but offer financial assistance. At Camberley in Surrey, a new edge-of-town site, Marks & Spencer were involved in moving a meadow so that wild flowers were preserved.

All new company cars take lead-free petrol, and, where technically possible, existing company cars have been converted. The public is well aware of the extent to which transport figures in the drive towards a better environment. Marks & Spencer has pioneered the development of the 'quiet delivery vehicle'. So far achievements include reduction of trailer noise and unloading noise by fitting air suspension and noise-suppressant floors in the trailers and quietening the tail lifts. Our hauliers operate high levels of servicing so that there are no 'dirty' lorries with cloud emissions. Most vehicles are now replaced every three years.

Marks & Spencer's energy-saving survey has saved £50 million over fourteen years. On the subject of energy conservation it has to be said that the responsibility of every business and of each individual citizen is more vital today than it has ever been. That responsibility took on a new and sombre aspect following the

Yom Kippur War in 1973 and the decision of the OPEC countries
to restrict the supply of oil to the West, causing steep price
increases and releasing an unprecedented spiral of inflation. In
the summer of 1974 the British Government called for a 10% cut
in the consumption of energy. I decided to respond at once.

Although Marks & Spencer is not a huge user of power, it
does, however, use considerable amounts in lighting and heating
the stores, and in ensuring that the refrigeration and chilled
counters operate efficiently. I wrote to the chairman of the 'Think
Tank' at that time, Victor Rothschild, asking him whether the
'Think Tank' had any suggestions for using electricity more
efficiently. I received a three word reply 'Switch It Off'. Within
a fortnight we had over 20,000 of these signs beneath every light
switch in the business.

We then discussed with Phillips, the Dutch electrical firm,
whether they had any suggestions. They said they had just
invented a new TL84 fluorescent lighting tube which they claimed
would give the same light intensity using only 80% of the electricity that the present lighting used, but it had never been tried
commercially. We made an experiment which was very successful.
The light intensity was maintained and the saving in electricity
was somewhere between 15% and 20%. Over the next eighteen
months we equipped every store with these new lighting tubes.
The managing director of Phillips told me we had over 200 miles
of their lighting tubes in our stores. Meanwhile we found that
we could heat floors, whether they were sales floors or stockroom
floors, partially or fully from the heat exhausted from the refriger-
ator counters. As we experimented, we found many other ways
of making economies in the consumption of fuel, including
improved insulation, without impairing the efficiency of our
operation. In each store and at head office we established an
energy conservation team to ensure that initial savings were
maintained and, where possible, increased. Our first year's savings

in 1974 were approximately £500,000. Since then, as I said, we estimate that we have saved approximately £50 million by more effective use of the energy we need to run the stores, warehouses, cold counters, etc. I cannot think of any three words which have paid bigger dividends in every sense than Lord Rothchild's 'Switch It Off'.

One of the ways in which Marks & Spencer's sense of responsibility to the community operates in Britain or overseas is our policy of seeking to *source* in the UK. Wherever possible the goods we sell are produced in the British Isles, and we try to do this so far as we can in all other countries in which we operate. 85% of the clothing sold in Marks & Spencer is manufactured in the UK. People used to say that it would be cheaper to buy many of the goods we sold in other countries, in the Far East, for example. However, we have acted on the premise that close co-operation with British suppliers and the encouragement of efficient methods of production would enable us to sell more home produced goods representing high quality and good value, and for which there would be a growing demand. We thought, too, that being near our suppliers would be an advantage in solving any problems which might arise and in developing new products. These beliefs have turned out to be well founded, and we have derived great benefit from applying them. So, too, have the customers and the community.

In chapter seven, as an instance of developing production at home, I described how Dewhirst started to produce men's suits for Marks & Spencer and, as a result, created 1,000 jobs. Another example is that of Tim Tinsley and his vegetables. Twenty years or so ago all the carrots which Marks & Spencer sold in the summer season were imported from Holland. The Dutch carrot was called the Amsterdam Forcing Carrot and had the justified reputation of being the best in Europe. I suggested we should grow this Dutch carrot in England, but was told by experts that it would not flourish in British soil. Nevertheless, our own technologist thought it could be grown in Britain. We eventually found the late Tim Tinsley, a Lincolnshire farmer of great ability with a 2,000-acre farm, who believed he could grow this particular variety.

He was as good as his word. The Tinsley carrot was at least as good as the Dutch carrot, and certainly no more expensive. Tinsley went on to produce other vegetables which he processed for us into prepared salads. When we first met Tim, he employed twenty people on the farm; the Tinsley farm now employs some 1,250 people and covers 4,000 acres. As a farm it is outstanding and its processing plants are of the highest standards. Since it cannot always meet the growing demand, it subcontracts to neighbouring farmers, thereby creating further employment. Marks & Spencer's turnover with Tinsley runs into tens of millions of pounds.

It has been Marks & Spencer's policy when we develop substantial business with overseas suppliers to encourage them, if it can be made profitable for them, to set up plants in the United Kingdom. Eleven such plants have been set up. Delta of Israel have established a plant in Lesmahagow, just south of Glasgow, where unemployment was 18%; this now has 200 employees and is profitable. Rahbefisk, a Danish company who are Marks & Spencer's major fish supplier, have set up a plant in Redditch; the number of employees there has grown in the last five years from about 50 to 220.

I wrote earlier about how difficult it had been for us to get men's suits produced in the United Kingdom, with the result that we had to import from Italy, Scandinavia and Israel. After a while we encouraged our Israeli supplier, Bagir, to set up a finishing plant for their suits in the United Kingdom. They established it in Lancashire, where it has been a success, and now employs approximately 400 staff.

I have a very agreeable personal recollection of how one overseas company came to set up a plant in the UK. For many years I went annually to stay with a childhood friend, Freddie Brisson, and his wife, film star Rosalind Russell, in Los Angeles. They had a wonderful cook and when one day we had a particularly delicious cake, I said to 'Roz', 'I know your cook is very good, but I didn't know she could produce a cake like this.' 'Don't be silly,' she replied, 'this is a frozen cake I bought at the supermarket.' She showed me the package: the brand name was Sara Lee. I found out it was produced in a bakery in Chicago, so I arranged with the owner, Charlie Lubin, to visit him on my way back home.

Charlie Lubin's operation was most impressive: a superb bakery, spotlessly clean, with first-class equipment and high-quality raw materials. All his products were excellent, and most were frozen. The following night I found myself at dinner sitting next to Nate Cummings, the head of a large group called Consolidated Foods. I had known Nate for several years.

'I hear you visited the Sara Lee kitchens yesterday. What did you think of them?'

'Why do you ask?' I replied.

'Well, we've bought Sara Lee. What do you think we should do with it?'

'Is it profitable?' I asked.

'Very.'

I said, 'Then let it carry on as it is. You are an entrepreneur with a huge food business, but you know nothing about bakeries. Let Charlie Lubin continue to run it.' Nate did so.

For many years Nate and Charlie wanted Marks & Spencer to take Sara Lee products. I said we would make a trial providing we were told what ingredients went into the cakes and that we would be free to sell them under the St Michael name. Nate Cummings would not accept this; they did no private label production, and were not prepared to start. We did not let the possibility drop, however, and it came up from time to time between us for the next twenty years. At last, when he was about eighty, Nate Cummings said, 'Marcus, I think our board would agree to produce under the "St Michael" name, but if we did, we would have to have below "St Michael" a little label "By the Kitchens of Sara Lee"'. I said, 'No – if we agreed that, what would our other food suppliers who produce special "St Michael" items for Marks and Spencer say? They'd want the same.' Then, one day, Nate came back to me. His board had conceded the point, and so we placed a substantial trial order. The cakes were produced in Chicago, flown to the UK and were sold at the price we would have put on them if they had been produced in the UK.

The cakes sold well. Consolidated Foods then bought an old, rather dilapidated bakery in Yorkshire, employing some sixty people, rebuilt and modernized it, and in the UK we became their main customer. Their operation here has been a success, and has led to the creation of some 600 jobs.

In all, our overseas suppliers who set up plants for producing in the UK employ some 4,000 people. Of course they do not only produce for us, but we are in some cases their sole customer. I appreciate that these increases in employment are modest, but, if other firms were willing and able to apply the same sourcing policy, the effect of reducing unemployment would be substantial.

In 1983 I was invited by Roger Milliken, one of the largest, if not the largest, private fabric manufacturer in the United States, to talk at the annual meeting of the American Textile Manufacturers Institute, which was held at the famous Greenbriars Hotel in West Virginia. The convention was attended by leading textile manufacturers of the United States and by many other influential business leaders who had interests in textiles. Roger Milliken had invited me primarily to talk about Marks & Spencer's home sourcing policy. Before accepting I asked him why he wanted me to lay emphasis in my speech on this particular subject. His answer was: 'If enough American retailers don't adopt a similar policy, the textile manufacturing industry in America can and probably will virtually disappear over the next ten years. The consequent increase in unemployment would run into hundreds of thousands.'

I said, 'Roger, you imply you would close your plants down. Surely you wouldn't do that?'

'Marcus, it might well come to that. If retailers over the next few years don't change their policies and try to source at home, many of my plants, if not all, could be closed and I would have to start manufacturing overseas, mainly in the Far East.'

So I decided to go to Greenbriars. I began by outlining my central belief:

Today there can only be real leadership in industry if top management understands the importance of implementing a policy of good human relations at work and if we in the West, in order to solve some of the increasing economic problems which we face, also understand our social responsibilities in and to the community, and act accordingly. ...

Providing one has the right philosophy and principles, it is possible to achieve results in the economic field, certainly in the United Kingdom, which many people believed were beyond the country's capacity. I believe this experience has application to your great country also.

I briefly recounted the history of Marks & Spencer, outlined the basic principles on which we had worked, our experience, our aspirations, where we had succeeded and where we had failed. I then delivered the message for which Roger had asked me:

We support home production and, wherever possible, we buy British made goods and foodstuffs – not blindly, but with patience and perseverance, co-operating closely with our suppliers, to ensure that what they produce represents quality and value. We do not seek protection from imports.

One of our principles is to give top priority to British production in all areas. 85% plus of what we sell is produced in the UK. This includes foodstuffs as well as clothing and home furnishings.

In buying British I want to make it clear that there is no point in buying British if the quality and value are not right. That has no future. We found, providing we were persistent and patient, much could be achieved in co-operation with manufacturers and many imports successfully and profitably replaced by home production.

About eighteen months later Roger Milliken asked me to go to Bentonville, Arkansas, the headquarters of Wal-Mart Stores, the most successful chain of its type in the United States. Roger wanted me to talk to Sam Walton, the founder and head of Wal-Mart and his executives and managers. The subject once again was Marks & Spencer's policies with emphasis on sourcing in the United Kingdom. There were about 200 people present. I delivered my message and then answered questions for an hour and a half. At the end of the session Mr Walton declared he now intended to follow the example of Marks & Spencer and buy as much as he could in the USA. Soon after my visit, he sent some of his chief executives to London to visit our head office and learn how we operate in general as well as in relation to our home sourcing policy. We gave them such help as we could. In the last four years Wal-Mart has replaced imports to a value exceeding $1.5 billion with goods produced in the USA. They have created innumerable jobs for American citizens, many of whom had till then been unemployed.

In a long and highly complimentary article in the American

magazine *National Business*, which praises the efficiency and enlightment of the Wal-Mart organization, and especially their policy of good human relations at work, the following passages occur:

As in the American economy as a whole, in recent years a high percentage of Wal-Mart's merchandise had come from foreign manufacturers. Imports have accounted for perhaps 40% of Wal-Mart's sales – 4% to 5% in direct Wal-Mart imports and about 35% from American suppliers who have bought overseas.

Late in 1984 the torrent of imports began to weigh on Sam Walton. 'I had just finished a trip to Central America,' he recalls, 'and on the trip, something got to me about feeling that we needed to do all we could as a corporation to start buying merchandise in the United States, proving that we could be competitive.'

In March 1985 Sam Walton sent an open letter to US manufacturers, inviting them to take part in a 'Buy American' programme, and offering to work with them to produce goods that were competitive, in price and quality, with imports.

'Our American suppliers', Walton wrote, 'must commit to improving their facilities and machinery, remain financially conservative and work to fill our requirements and, most importantly, strive to improve employee productivity.' Wal-Mart believes our American workers can make the difference if management provides the leadership.

'The best part', of Buy American, Sam Walton says, 'as important as any other, is to try to get our manufacturers to create a partnership with their workers the way we've tried to do with our people, and share the profits with them.' Wal-Mart, he says, is encouraging its vendors 'to do a better job of managing, and a better job of relating to the workers. We invite them to come and talk to us about how we measure productivity, the way we've set up goals and incentives.'

Although they are fiercely competitive, Walton and his colleagues know that their company owes its success less to its competitive drive than to how well it has cultivated every possible community of interest – with its employees, its customers and, now, its suppliers.

Through 'Buy American' Wal-Mart is telling American manufacturers that they can strengthen their place in the world economy by making themselves more like Wal-Mart – that is, by embracing a corporate philosophy that finds the greatest value not in profits alone, but in profits through a harmonious striving together.

In the last six years Wal-Mart's sales have increased from $6,401 million in 1984 to over $20 billion in 1989. Profits after tax have increased from $271 million in 1984 to $1,075 million in 1989. The business trades from 1,565 stores and employs 223,000 staff.

I believe that the policy of sourcing as far as possible at home is not just to the advantage of the country concerned but also to international trade, provided sourcing at home is based on good value and not on high tariffs. If unemployment at home is reduced, people at work have more money to spend and some of this goes on imports. Much of it will go on holidays abroad, and tourism today is one of the fastest growing industries in the world.

In chapter six I described Operation Simplification, which led to the elimination of 26 million pieces of paper per year and greatly improved the efficiency of Marks & Spencer's operations. We were so pleased with the success of the exercise that we thought as many of our staff as possible should know all about it, so we set up an exhibition to describe and illustrate its background and its fruition. It was originally intended for our employees of all grades but a number of people outside the company expressed a desire to visit it. So we made our exhibition public, seeing this as an opportunity to accept a responsibility to the community.

One of our visitors was a very senior person from the Ministry of Defence. When he had seen it, he said to me, 'I am envious of what you are doing. I'd like to think we could have a similar examination of the administrative procedures of the Armed Forces. Nowadays we virtually have a full enquiry if a pair of boots disappears from the stocks.' I do not know what, if anything, happened when he got back to his office, but soon afterwards the Prime Minister of the day visited the Simplification exhibition and subsequently requested that several senior civil servants should spend time at our head office learning how we had implemented the operation and how far our results could be applied to Government administration.

For a firm – and indeed for an individual – to accept responsibility towards the community sometimes requires sacrifice. One evening early in 1970, before he became Prime Minister, Ted Heath, the leader of the Conservative Party, asked ten people to dinner at his flat in Albany. The only politician present apart from our host was Robert Carr; the other guests were from industry and commerce, among them the chairman of Unilever, the chairman of Rio Tinto Zinc and one of the senior directors of Shell Oil. The dinner was delicious and the wine so outstanding that I asked to see the bottle; I remember to this day that it was Cheval Blanc '45. When dinner was finished, Ted Heath made a short speech, saying that when he became Prime Minister it was his intention that his Government would work more closely with industry than any of its predecessors. To make this co-operation effective he wanted each of us to second to Government for a minimum of two years a top-class person from our businesses.

He asked one of his guests what he thought of the idea. 'Well it's a good idea, Ted, but we couldn't afford to second anybody for two years from our main board, though I'm sure we could find someone down the line in one of our subsidiaries for this job.'

I decided to intervene: 'Your first-class dinner, excellent talk, good idea and outstanding wine will be wasted if, having decided to support your Government, we don't loan it the people we can't really afford.'

I went back to the office and spoke to Teddy Sieff and Father. I said there were three people in Marks & Spencer who might be able to do the job: Jan Lewando, Derek Rayner or myself (I have never been modest). Since I would shortly be taking on more responsibilities in the business, and Jan, who was older than me, was getting on, I said I thought our choice for the secondment, if he were agreeable, should be Derek Rayner.

'What have you done?' asked Teddy. 'You can't commit us like that.'

'We have a responsibility to the country,' I retorted. 'We must respond positively to Ted Heath's request. I *have* committed us and I think Derek Rayner, if he is willing, should go.'

Derek Rayner was indeed willing and, when Ted Heath became Prime Minister after the Conservatives won the 1970 General Election, Derek joined him. Initially he had a roving commission to look at the administration side of Government generally, but then he was asked to examine defence procurement and make recommendations. When I asked him why he had agreed to concentrate on one Ministry only, he replied, 'I cannot examine all the Ministries and do a worthwhile job, and I think that if I concentrate on one Ministry and do something worthwhile there, perhaps other Ministries will follow.'

He completed his assignment within a year and made recommendations. Lord Carrington, who was then Minister of Defence, said to him: 'Having made these recommendations, I suggest that you now try to implement them.' Derek did so, successfully. Lord Carrington told me that he had done an excellent job and had set an example for other Ministries to follow.

After the Conservative Government was defeated in 1974 and

Labour took over, Harold Wilson, the new Prime Minister, asked Derek if he would stay on and help, which he did for another year. When Mrs Thatcher became Prime Minister in 1979, she requested that Derek should again be seconded to advise on improving efficiency and eliminating waste in Government departments. Derek made a major contribution to the improvement of efficient Government management between 1979 and 1983, and saved the taxpayers hundreds of millions of pounds.

The majority of the other business leaders at Ted Heath's dinner did not second to Government any of their first-class people. In general those they supplied were of limited ability or may once have been very good but had got a bit past it; certainly they lasted only a relatively short time in their Government jobs. I think their companies lost out in consequence. Marks & Spencer gained. Derek learned a good deal – what was well done in Government, and what poorly. I think his experience in Whitehall helped him to make a significant contribution to the leadership of Marks & Spencer since he became chairman in 1984.

I mentioned earlier the high standards of Bovis's policy of good human relations at work. Their sense of responsibility to the community is also of the highest. Such standards, inevitably, begin at the top. A fine example at the time of writing is the work Bovis is doing at Hyde Park Corner in London, where the old St George's Hospital has been vacated and is being gutted. Within the old shell Bovis are building a prestigious hotel and office block, a major building project. I pass this site most evenings on my way home from the office and I see that, in spite of all the building work, how outstandingly tidy and clean the site is kept no matter what the weather is like. I went into the site one day unannounced and was shown round by a junior manager. The standards were high. I wrote to congratulate Roger Mabey, the director concerned. Subsequently, he invited me to visit the site with him for a thorough tour. Despite all the construction work being carried out, the interior of the site was being kept as clean and tidy as the periphery.

If people individually and businesses generally tried to maintain standards as high as Bovis's there would be fewer criticisms by foreign tourists of the poor standard of cleanliness and increasing quantities of litter on our streets. These shabby standards are beginning to have an adverse effect on our tourist trade, which is an important invisible export. It is sad to have to say that the adverse balance of trade in tourism was nearly £1 billion sterling in 1988 and is growing worse, especially since tourism world-wide is probably the largest and fastest growing international export today. Michael Medlicott, the British Tourist Authority's chief executive, said, 'High prices, poor domestic transport and dirty leisure facilities threaten the growth of tourist industries in the 1990s. Britain is in danger of both pricing and dirtying itself out of its place among the world's top five tourist countries.' The British Tourist Authority announced that after another record year for tourism in 1988, when 15.9m overseas residents visited the UK and spent £4.6 billion, excluding air fares, it expected tourist numbers to rise another 25% by 1993 to 19.9 million, with the amount spent going up to over £10 billion. 'But', said Mr Medlicott, 'unacceptable levels of litter and pollution' could lead to a lower growth rate.

Recently a friend of my wife's who lives in Vienna came to stay with us with her small child. It was the first time they had visited London. One evening I asked her what she was going to do the following day. She replied she was going to do a tour of London, see the sights. I asked her if she would like a car to take her around. No, she said, she was going to take a ride on the official open-deck tourist bus and listen to the guide's expert commentary. When she came back, I asked her how she had enjoyed her trip. She replied: 'London is a fascinating city to tour, but I would never travel on one of those official buses again. The deck where the tourists sit is a disgrace – dirty and full of litter. I wouldn't have stayed on it if I had not wanted so much to see and learn about London. But I shall make sure to warn any friends of mine who are coming to London not to use the official buses.'

It is, of course, the responsibility of the individual not to litter our streets, not only in our cities but in country areas also. It is the responsibility of the local authority concerned to see that there are adequate receptacles, bins, etc., into which litter can be placed. But one has only to walk around most of our cities and beauty spots in the countryside to see litter, cigarette ends, paper bags, etc., being dropped.

It is the responsibility of those in charge of business, no matter what they are, to set an example by ensuring high standards of cleanliness and tidiness in their workplace, providing adequate facilities in which to deposit their litter and rubbish. They should seek to observe standards similar to the ones that Bovis has maintained for the last two years on their Hyde Park Corner development site. If we could implement nationally a policy of this sort, it would make for a more pleasant environment in which to live and work. Such a policy must come from the top, and everyone right down the line should be encouraged to implement it. It is part of the responsibility of business to the community.

Finally, on this question of responsibility to the community, I would like to mention United Biscuits. Under Sir Hector Laing, United Biscuits has been among the leaders in committing funds, management time and staff involvement to community projects. The company has been an innovator, setting an example which others have followed. Eight or so years ago Hector Laing and

Mark Weinberg, the well-known city financier, founded the Percent Club. Those who wished to join the club would promise to allocate 1% of business pre-tax profits to community projects. Some who joined the club were not prepared to donate 1%, but, as a result of the Hector Laing-Mark Weinberg initiative, substantial sums have been raised and support for the club is growing.

United Biscuits has set splendid examples particularly in union–management consultation and co-operation, seeking to provide maximum possible security of employment and optimum job satisfaction with the delegation of responsibility. Sir Hector has done marvellous work in communication. During his visits to United Biscuits' factories he personally talks to about half the workforce in the UK, over 40,000, in groups of anything from 20 to 200, covering all shifts. Among the important messages he has succeeded in getting across to employees is that it is ultimately the customer, not the employer, who pays the wages. The customer demands quality and value, so it is only if employer and employee work as a team that they will beat the competition to win and keep customers, thus securing their own jobs.

United Biscuits has always respected the role of the trade unions and, by maintaining an ongoing dialogue with union officials in good times and bad, has established sound working relationships with them. As long as twenty years ago the company took the initiative in establishing an agreement with its biggest unions, General Municipal Boiler Makers Allied Trade Union and the Union of Shops, Distributives and Allied Workers, providing national negotiating rights against the background of the agreed objective, namely:

> *to meet the natural desire of people for an increasing standard of living,*
> *but to achieve this objective to the greatest extent possible by continuous*

improvement in productivity rather than by passing increased wage costs on in the form of price increases which will adversely affect both the interest of the consumer and the competitive position of the company's products.

The key to United Biscuits' success with trade union leaders and with workers on the shop floor – the two do not invariably go together – is not found in written agreements but in the trust built up over many years between the company and its employees' representatives. The company is very open in explaining its business performance at all levels, and regular meetings are held between the managing directors of the operating companies and the union national officers to discuss how things are going. In particular, many constructive developments have been achieved by joint company/union working parties, dealing with, among other things, job evaluation, procedures for handling technological change, sick pay, and reorganization of working practices. All concerned have invested patience and good will, with the result that there is a strong commitment on both sides to make the changes work.

Amicable working relationships have been put to severe test by the closure of major factories, necessitated by over-capacity in the biscuit industry. After the advance announcement of the closure of United Biscuits' factory in Liverpool, the unions were given full access to the company's accounts to enable them, if they wished, to prepare and submit a plan for dealing with the problem different from the one the company had drawn up. The unions' alternative was duly submitted and discussed. It did not prove workable, but the discussions and negotiations which followed were based on sincerely constructive attempts by all concerned to help the people affected by the closures by means of retraining, redeployment, assistance with outplacement and financial support from the company for community and job creation initiatives.

It is encouraging to be able to record that, as is usually the case, these practices and initiatives, good for the employees, good for the community, have also been very good for United Biscuits' profits. By obtaining employee commitment to the objectives of the business through good human relations, the company has been able to reduce unit labour costs, introduce new technology without opposition, and substantially restructure operations and working practices. This has ensured continuity of supply to customers, as well as better value for money.

United Biscuits has produced a booklet entitled 'Ethics and Operating Principles' and the following is extracted from it:

United Biscuits' business ethics are not negotiable – a well-founded reputation for scrupulous dealing is itself a priceless company asset and the most important single factor in our success is faithful adherence to our beliefs. While our tactical plans and many other elements constantly change, our basic philosophy does not. To meet the challenges of a changing world we are prepared to change everything about ourselves except our values.

I hope all employees will feel proud to be identified with a company which sets high standards of business conduct and expects everyone to live up to them.

We believe in and obey both the letter and the spirit of the law, but the law is the minimum and no set of rules can provide all the answers or cover all questionable situations. While it is the responsibility of top management to keep a company honest and honorable, perpetuating ethical values is not a function only of the chief executive or a handful of senior managers. Every employee is expected to take on the responsibility of always behaving ethically whatever the circumstances. Beliefs and values must always come before policies, practices and goals; the latter must be altered if they violate fundamental beliefs.

To endure, a company must serve all those who have an interest in it. United Biscuits wants to have solid lasting relationships with its shareholders, employees and franchisees, with customers and suppliers, with the communities where we live and work and with Governments and the public at large. It is our policy always to deal with all our constituencies fairly, responsibly and with integrity.

We rely on our staff as individuals to practise the highest moral and ethical standards in all our business activities. We as individuals must so conduct ourselves as to contribute towards the integrity of the company as a whole. People at every level in the business must be encouraged to make known any issues that may raise or appear to raise a potential problem and to review with senior management any issue that might be of questionable ethical standard.

We place the highest priority on promoting and preserving the health and safety of employees. Employees, for their part, have a clear duty to take every reasonable precaution to avoid injury to themselves, their colleagues and members of the public.

Customers

Both employees and customers need to know that products sold by any of our operating companies will always meet their highest expectations. The integrity of our products is sacrosanct and implicit in this commitment is an absolute and uncompromising dedication to quality. We will never compromise on recipes or specification of product in order to save costs. Quality improvement must always be our goal.

Competitors

We compete vigorously, energetically, untiringly but we also compete ethically and honestly. Our competitive success is founded on excellence – of product and service. We have no need to disparage our competitors either directly or by implication or innuendo.

I end this chapter with this thought: business, like an individual, should carry out its responsibility to the community as a moral obligation. Just as an employer should believe it is his duty to promote good human relations, so too he should see it as a duty to pursue the best possible relationship with the community, a relationship inspired by the notion of giving, not just taking. There is a reward, however, for employers who practise such a policy in that spirit: the first to perceive and to respond to this policy will be the community itself. Good works will be rewarded – as I showed earlier – not only by support, but also by good publicity, ranging from word of mouth to reports in the mass media. And, if I may end with a word for the cynics who believe nothing should be done unless it is profitable, responsibility to the community will enhance, not diminish, the bottom line.

ten

LOOKING TO THE FUTURE

Everybody who reads this book will have seen how much importance I attach to all management, from the top downwards, implementing a policy of good human relations at work and of business responsibility to the community. Some businessmen will say that I attach too much importance to both these principles.

Other business leaders sometimes object that the kind of good human relations policy which I advocate in this book, though it may be relevant to those who work in shops or in similar employment is not relevant to those who work in manufacturing industry or in comparable activity. In other words, a policy good for shop or restaurant staff is not necessarily good for a steel plant, oil rig or heavy industry.

Such criticism is misguided. What is good in essence and in principle for the shopkeeper is good for the coalminer, what is good for the waitress is good for the cleaning lady, and what is good for all those is good for the operator working alongside dozens of others or on his own in a huge room full of computers. The essentials and principles are what count, and the essentials and principles do not vary.

The key fact about a policy of good human relations at work is that it is not *primarily* concerned with the nature of the work which the employee does but with the state of mind, the spirit in

which he or she does it. A policy of good human relations at
work is not about jobs, it is about people. There is no better
example than the British motor car industry. I have described in
chapter five the disaster and the cost to the nation of the tough
personnel policy which Leonard Lord tried to implement when
he led the British Motor Corporation (BMC), ignoring a policy
of good human relations. Instead of getting the workers' co-
operation, his policy infuriated them, which often resulted in
industrial strife, strikes and left-wing trouble makers seizing authority in the unions with disastrous results for BMC. Although
Donald Stokes and Michael Edwardes, I am sure, tried to rectify
this, they inherited an enormous problem which has led to a
disastrous performance by the British car industry. Despite some
improvements in recent years, the adverse trade balance in the
imports of cars over exports was £6.1 billion in 1988, and will
be substantial again in 1989. At the same time, we see that the
Nissan car factory recently established in Sunderland is making
excellent progress and that this is partly due to the implementation
of a policy of good human relations at work throughout the
plant.

Another common objection is that people like me talk as
though only a handful of business leaders follow a policy of good
human relations at work today, whereas, say my critics, good
policies have in fact become the rule, not the exception in Britain
and the United States today. Believe me, I wish that were so. I
pay full tribute to those many companies whose success in this
field deserve nothing but praise. I have cited several outstanding
examples earlier in this book. I know from the conferences I am
asked to address here and overseas, particularly in the United
States, and from private meetings with business leaders who want
to improve their relations with their employees that more firms
every year have seen the light and are trying to establish sound
policies on a firm on-going basis. But many companies have a

long way to go, and there is still a large number of companies who seem indifferent to what is required. What is worse, I could name cases where, though there was once progress, there is now reaction. I could, alas, name firms who have used the severely competitive operating conditions in British business today as an excuse for cutting back on many of their social programmes. Plans relevant to the improvement of human relations at work and to the practice of business responsibility to the community are frequently the first to suffer despite the fact that knowledge, foresight and enlightened self-interest tell us that they should be the last to go as the experiences (cited earlier) of wise companies like Bovis, United Biscuits, Sony and Wal-Mart clearly demonstrate.

How shortsighted about their own interests the reactionaries are! But then, if they had been well and imaginatively led, if they had learned the lessons of history, they would probably not have got into trouble in the first place.

I now come to the main purpose of this final chapter, which is to dwell on an aspect of the need for a vigorous policy of good human relations at work which I have not explored earlier in this book, though some of what I want to say is implicit in it.

Throughout the book, when speaking of good human relations policies, I have emphasised on the one hand the *moral* desirability of these and on the other the *economic* desirability. Now I deal with the social, if not the *political*, desirability.

We are all conscious of the tensions which are created by unemployment. However, tensions can also be created by employment, even full employment. Too much tension in the working day of millions of people is socially and politically damaging. People who go home tense at the end of the day can be troublesome. They may be irritable with their spouses or children, have quarrels, even fights, or they may sit silently and sullenly, creating an atmosphere not of relaxation but of edginess and resentment, if not of outright animosity. Such a way of ending the day is not productive; it is enervating and abrasive. It takes a toll on the nerves; it prevents even the healing balm of a good night's sleep; and it can even lead to illness, nervous breakdown. We read frequently about the number of working hours lost by individuals suffering from back trouble, the symptoms often being due more to mental rather than physical strain. So, as well as being bad for the individual worker, his family and friends face tension, stress or strain – whatever the name given to it – at home.

Alternatively, at the end of the day the strung-up, fraught employee may try to escape from tensions by anaesthetizing himself with a few drinks, by burying himself morosely in an evening paper or by staring without much real interest or comprehension at a television screen, whilst his wife follows suit either to keep the precarious peace or because she cannot think of anything better to do in the circumstances. Such escapism is not healthy personally, socially or, indeed, politically. Indeed, it could be and has been politically dangerous. In the extreme, but not unheard-of, case this kind of need to escape was a factor in the growth of German Fascism. It was part of that emotional surge which overwhelmed the audiences at near-hysterical Nazi rallies and of the frenzied adulation which poured out towards the Führer. It contributes to the mood which hopelessly and dispiritedly tolerates repressive Communism. In cases not so exreme it can breed the sort of intolerance and short temper which can feed, even engender, class conflict, political militancy and racism, because people who begin to feel they are not cared for may themselves cease to care. They become resentful and may consequently become aggressive, not necessarily consciously and perhaps not overtly. But the attitude will be there and will be dangerous. It may express itself in political attitudes, not necessarily in Nazism, but perhaps in militant trade union activities of a kind more political than industrial. In any case, a policy of care and consideration on the part of employers which is manifested in a consistent and patient policy of good human relations at work is the best way of de-politicizing feelings and attitudes which, if fed into political activity, open or concealed, can have a disruptive effect on the affairs of the community.

A thoroughgoing pervasive – and persuasive – policy of good human relations in the workplace can make a contribution not only to the contentment and welfare of the employees in their jobs, and to the efficiency and profitability of the company, but also to the prevailing mood of society in general. Think for a moment about the difference between a society in which the employees go home tired, tense, resentful and, perhaps, with a sense of being 'us' unjustly treated by 'them', of being overworked and uncared for by the bosses, and on the other hand a society in which employees return home with the feeling that they have done a fulfilling day's work which, though its demands have fatigued them, has left them with a healthy anticipation and desire for an evening of relaxation and enjoyment – as well as a reasonable amount of wages with which to pay for it. This is an oversimplification, but I think it is one which does not distort the facts and which points a moral.

If this line of thought is valid, it points to the degree of responsibility which our business leaders have, whether they know it or not, for the kind of society in which they operate, which indeed in part they create, and for the kind of society which may be just ahead. The inspiration must come from the top. If our business leaders and our managements face this, decide to make every effort to have contented, co-operative and loyal employees, and are seen to be at least trying to achieve this – that is all important – they are bound to have a beneficial influence on the kind of society they and their employees are living in.

Perhaps some of our social and political problems can be solved more effectively through better working conditions and a pleasant social atmosphere at the workplace created by employers than through the laws, rules and regulations created by our politicians. Possibly the frontiers of the state could be rolled back in yet another area of our activities: enlightened business leadership taking the place of Government.

Businessmen are often critical of trade union activities. Some years ago, when the general secretary of the Union of Construction, Allied Trades and Technicians, Les Wood, was on the panel at the national conference of the National Federation of Building Trades Employers he made a statement to the effect that, if *all* leaders behaved as enlightened and responsible business leaders do then he and other trade union leaders would be out of a job, he may have been indulging in lighthearted exaggeration, but the point he made gives serious food for thought.

The Confederation of British Industry employers' conference held in London on the 11 November 1989 heard that a study of thirty-six organizations had found strong correlations between the way in which organizations operated and staff turnover and absenteeism. There is also a proven relationship between absenteeism and the degree of stress individuals encounter from the way their work is organized and the amount of support they receive from others. Professor Cox of Nottingham University, told the conference that the degree of help individuals received in solving work problems was an accurate predictor of absenteeism levels. Retraining and career development courses, and working in teams to solve problems all helped reduce levels of stress. Companies that were organized in this way had less absence from work and were also perceived as good organizations for which to work. Professor Cox also pointed out that absence due to stress cost industry ten times more than industrial disputes, and that

British levels of absence were double those in some European countries.

One often hears such remarks as, 'Keep politics out of business,' or even the reverse, 'Keep business out of politics.' In one sense it is desirable to do both of these things, but in another sense it is impossible. It is sensible that governments should leave business decisions to businessmen and not require businessmen to take measures which are political. But if political leaders commit themselves to national economic policies which result in millions of people becoming unemployed or, on the other hand, to social programmes which maintain full or nearly full employment at the cost of inflation escalating to 25%, how can politics be kept out of business or business be kept out of politics?

It is a combination of the guidance of the businessman and the energy of the co-operative worker, and not the State, which should create the national wealth necessary to provide real social progress, proper social security and true social care. To create such wealth employer and employee must co-operate with the minimum of Government interference. All this must be achieved with the businessman carrying out his responsibilities as a caring citizen and a loyal, considerate employer.

For many years British businessmen – and indeed businessmen in other countries including the United States – have complained that successive governments (irrespective of their political affiliations) and trade unions have restricted their activities and have forced upon them hampering regulations in many fields, including their treatment of their employees. However, many of these same businessmen would agree that life has been made easier for them today as a result of some of the legislative changes over the past few years, reform of trade union law, for instance.

In my view the remedy for too much Government restriction and regulation, especially in the field of what is still referred to as 'industrial relations', is in the businessman's own hands. If enough leading businessmen are seen to be caring employers, there will soon be less need for laws or Government regulations to restrict their activities and protect the interests of their employees. Also, if they give more to the community, they will need to be taxed less.

In taking on new responsibilities for the well-being of their employees business leaders should not fear being described as 'paternalistic'. There are some British firms who rejoice in that epithet, and their record of relations with their workers and their profitability suggest that there is nothing wrong with paternalism if it is realistic, fair, open and benign.

The fact is that Western society is in need of new attitudes and fresh initiatives on the part of its business leaders; the old ones will not do. If business leaders will not take the lead in changing them, other people and other forces may make the changes for them, and do so in a manner and to a degree which businessmen will not like. There is a new morality in the business world, new machines, new methods of production, new electronic processes, new standards, new thinking, new expectations on the part of the employee. This experience is still, unfortunately, confined to a minority, but that will change, and it is better for the others to help, hasten and control the process rather than let it happen to them.

If we businessmen accept the challenge to adapt to these new times and circumstances – and not only accept but lead – we shall not only have happier and more efficient employees, but better, more productive and more profitable businesses, and more satisfied shareholders; we shall also be helping to create a stronger, healthier, freer society in which much of the intervention by Government and trade unions deemed necessary even today will become out of date and unnecessary.

Employers and employees could then perhaps embrace the vision which idealistic Socialists and enlightened capitalists saw

many decades ago – a society characterized by humane and enterprising business leaders directing and rewarding the efforts of
energetic employees in open, enlightened and democratic partnership, based on the practice of good human relations at the
workplace, the practice of responsibility to the community, and
creating the wealth which is necessary to enable us all, locally and
nationally, to improve our standard of living through implementing a policy of care.

INDEX